AMOS IN TALMUD AND MIDRASH

A Source Book

Jacob Neusner

Studies in Judaism

University Press of America,® Inc.
Lanham · Boulder · New York · Toronto · Plymouth, UK

Copyright © 2007 by
University Press of America,® Inc.
4501 Forbes Boulevard
Suite 200
Lanham, Maryland 20706
UPA Acquisitions Department (301) 459-3366

Estover Road
Plymouth PL6 7PY
United Kingdom

All rights reserved
Printed in the United States of America
British Library Cataloging in Publication Information Available

Library of Congress Control Number: 2006931719
ISBN-13: 978-0-7618-3593-6 (paperback : alk. paper)
ISBN-10: 0-7618-3593-8 (paperback : alk. paper)

∞™ The paper used in this publication meets the minimum
requirements of American National Standard for Information
Sciences—Permanence of Paper for Printed Library Materials,
ANSI Z39.48—1984

Studies in Judaism

EDITOR

Jacob Neusner
Bard College

EDITORIAL BOARD

Alan J. Avery-Peck
College of the Holy Cross

Herbert Basser
Queens University

Bruce D. Chilton
Bard College

José Faur
Bar Ilan University

William Scott Green
University of Rochester

Mayer Gruber
Ben-Gurion University of the Negev

Günter Stemberger
University of Vienna

James F. Strange
University of South Florida

Contents

Preface vii

1. Amos in the Mishnah, tractate Abot, and the Tosefta 1

2. Amos in Sifra, the two Sifrés and Mekhilta Attributed to R. Ishmael 5

3. Amos in the Yerushalmi 25

4. Amos in Genesis Rabbah, Leviticus Rabbi, and Pesiqta deRab Kahana 35

5. Amos in Esther Rabbah I, Ruth Rabbah, Song of Songs Rabbah, and Lamentations rabbah. Abot deRabbi Natan 67

6. Amos in the Bavli 81

Index 119

Preface

> A language community is not just a group marked out by its use of a particular language: it is an evolving communion in its own right, whose particular view of the world is informed by a common language tradition. A language brings with it a mass of perceptions clichés, judgments and inspirations. In some sense, then, when one language replaces another, a people's view of the world must also be changing.
>
> Nicholas Ostler[1]

What happens to a religious community when its first language is replaced by a second, yet a third, and onward through time? Whether or not the new language marks a change in world-view remains to be seen. Continuities of culture despite variations of language demand deep deliberation. The communities that inherited the holy Scriptures of ancient Israel, Rabbinic Judaism and catholic, orthodox Christianity, found themselves possessed by divine writings in a language other than their own — writings dictated by God to prophets, for example. They nonetheless regarded themselves as those of and to whom in their day God through Scripture spoke, those that continued and now constituted the community of ancient Israel. And that was so even though they did not form a language community coherent with the language =of Scripture. But how to form a community of "perceptions, clichés, judgments and inspirations" within an alien yet authoritative language-world? Here is a case, common in religious traditions, in which one language replaces another even while the holy writings in the replaced language remain authoritative.

The Rabbinic sages of the first six centuries C.E. for their part recognized the difference between the language of Scripture and the language of the sages, that of the Mishnah for example. Greek and Latin, Aramaic and Syriac, Mishnaic or Middle Hebrew — none of the principal languages of Judaic and Christian antiquity opened the door to the received Scripture, which required translation. Yet all these language communities made their own the received writings in an alien tongue.

Theology trumps culture. For their heirs the ancient Israelite Scriptures represented authoritative accounts of God's messages in God's own wording. That is why the shift in language — from God's language, Hebrew as recorded by the prophets, to the languages of the faithful, now inheritors — challenged them to contemplate continuities from present to past. But they would say, from past to present. None could concede what is self-evident to modern historical linguistics, including devoted to Scripture: when one language replaces another, views of the world must also be changing. But how were authoritative writings in one language to be received by communities speaking a different language? Conveyed by a divine language that no one now spoke and that many did not comprehend, Scripture, its law and theology, history and prophecy, enjoyed the privileged position in the faith- and language-communities of Judaism and Christianity. Both religious traditions faced the task of mediating God's word of old to language-communities that used other words altogether to say other things entirely.

How they did so forms a principal problem in the study of formative Judaism and Christianity. In general terms, the Christian solution, the organization of the Old Testament and the New Testament, and the Judaic solution to the same problem, the formation of the doctrine of the dual Torah, an oral torah that amplified and complemented the written Torah of ancient Israel, run parallel. The New Testament found validation in the Old, as Christianity read backward from the Gospels to the Israelite prophets. The Rabbinic sages of the documents of the oral Torah received and recast the written one into wholly new modes of thought as well as of expression. They read forward from Scripture to the present moment. Nonetheless, that characterization of the reception of Scripture in formative Christianity and Judaism rests in general on examples and illustrations.

It is time for systematic work. This sourcebook and its companions represents the effort to collect and classify the hard facts in full detail of how Israelite Scripture was received and recast in the language-communities that produced the Bible in two Testaments of Christianity and the dual Torah of Judaism. Take the prophets, for example. Everyone knows that verses of prophecy figure prominently in the Gospels' narratives, and that they figure as proof-texts in Rabbinic exegesis of scriptural narratives as well. But to what end, and with what larger conception in mind? Biblical authority in Christianity forms a staple topic of theological inquiry. But I do not know of a systematic survey of how the Rabbinic *documents*, for their part, respond to the prophetic ones: select, explain, and utilize the received language of Scripture.

What is at stake in such a study is an account of how the Rabbinic system took over the prophetic writings and responded to their exhortations and theology — weighty issues. So far as prophetic Judaism challenges the covenantal nomism of Rabbinic Judaism, as some suppose it does, the wherewithal of evaluating that proposition, so critical to the history of Judaism, awaits. And these form only two important questions that a survey of Rabbinic readings of Israelite prophetic writings will help to resolve. This collection of Rabbinic comments on verses in the book of Amos carries forward the presentation of Jeremiah. It will be followed by anthologies of Rabbinic readings of Isaiah, Ezekiel, Hosea, and other prophets. I begin with the hypothesis that Rabbinic Judaism in its normative canon, from the Mishnah through the Bavli, not only formally through proof-texts but theologically through normative propositions represents a continuation and realization of Prophetic Judaism.

Preface ix

II

The Rabbinic sages of the first six centuries of the Common Era recognized that that Scripture's language was not their own, the Hebrew of the prophets and the Hebrew of the Mishnah and Midrash-compilations of Rabbinic Judaism being distinct forms of Hebrew. Here is a protracted account of their engagement with distinct linguistic usages and the meanings imputed to the differences, with italics signifying the use of Aramaic, plain type, of Hebrew:

Bavli Qiddushin 4:1-2 70a-b/V.5

A. *There was a man from Nehardea who went into a butcher shop in Pumbedita. He said to them, "Give me meat."*
B. *They said to him, "Wait until the servant of R. Judah bar Ezekiel gets his, and then we'll give to you."*
C. *He said, "So who is this Judah bar Sheviskel who comes before me to get served before me?"*
D. *They went and told R. Judah.*
E. He excommunicated him.
F. *They said, "He is in the habit of calling people slaves."*
G. *He proclaimed concerning him, "He is a slave."*
H. *The other party went and sued him in court before R. Nahman.*
I. *When the summons came, R. Judah went to R. Huna, he said to him, "Should I go, or shouldn't I go?"*
J. *He said to him, "In point of fact, you really don't have to go, because you are an eminent authority. But on account of the honor owing to the household of the patriarch [of the Babylonian Jews], get up and go."*
K. *He came. He found him making a parapet.*
L. *He said to him, "Doesn't the master concur with what R. Huna bar Idi said Samuel said,* 'Once a man is appointed administrator of the community, it is forbidden for him to do servile labor before three persons'?"
M. *He said to him, "I'm just making a little piece of the balustrade."*
N. *He said to him, "So what's so bad about the word, 'parapet,' that the Torah uses, or the word 'partition,' that rabbis use?"*
O. *He said to him, "Will the master sit down on a seat?"*
P. *He said to him, "So what's so bad about 'chair,' which rabbis use, or the word 'stool,' which people generally use?"*
Q. *He said to him, "Will the master eat a piece of citron-fruit?"*
R. *He said to him, "This is what Samuel said,* 'Whoever uses the word "citron-fruit" is a third puffed up with pride.' *It should be called either etrog, as the rabbis do, or 'lemony-thing,' as people do."*
S. *He said to him, "Would the master like to drink a goblet of wine?"*
T. *He said to him, "So what's so bad about the word 'wineglass,' as rabbis say, or 'a drink,' as people say?"*

The story further meanders in a variety of directions, but what is important for the present argument is clear: language-choices signaled social and cultural differences. Nor only so, but the use of Aramaic, rather than Hebrew, is attributed to God himself, by Jeremiah:

GENESIS RABBAH LXXIV:XIV.

1. A. "[Laban called it Jegar-sahadutha, but Jacob called it Galeed. Laban said, 'This heap is a witness between you and me today. Therefore he named it Galeed, and the pillar Mizpah, for he said, 'The Lord watch between you and me when we are absent one from the other. If you ill-treat my daughters or if you take wives besides my daughters, although no man is with us, remember, God is witness between you and me"']" (Gen. 31:47-50): "Laban called it Jegar-sahadutha:"
   B. Said R. Samuel bar Nahman, "Let the Aramaic language not be a minor one in your view, for in the Torah, the Prophets, and the Writings, the Holy One, blessed be he, paid all due respect to it.
   C. "In the Torah: 'Jegar-sahadutha.'
   D. "In the Prophets: 'Thus shall you say to them' (Jer. 10:11), [given in Aramaic].
   E. "In the Writings: 'Then spoke the Chaldeans to the king in Aramaic' (Dan. 2:4)."

The passage has God dictate to Jeremiah a prophesy in Aramaic, and this is a mark of the importance of that language.

How these differences in not only word choice but the entirety of language were sorted out affords perspective on the religious systems — Rabbinic Judaism, catholic, orthodox Christianity — that with Scripture in hand would emerge from late antiquity. The uses to which they put the heritage of the past reveal much about the traits of mind and theological program that characterized the heirs of Scripture. To be sure issues that provoke interest have tended to focus on whether the later generations impose upon the scriptural heritage their own concerns or attempt to replicate the original, historical message and perspective of the Scriptural writers. So Scripture as a historical resource has been made to stand in judgment upon the systematic theological readings of the heirs of Scripture in later times. But such a perspective imposes upon the Judaic sages and Christian theologians issues of historical authenticity that did not preoccupy them — they took for granted the historical facticity of Scripture's narratives and the authority of its laws — and obscures the issues that did concern them.

It is easier to invoke the notion that the sages and theologians possessed clear programs of inquiry, respectively, than exactly to define of what those programs consisted. It is common to impute to them issues important to contemporary learning, pertinent to, if not historical, then theological or philological-exegetical topics. So debates in the Judaic framework pursue the issues of whether exegesis is provoked

Preface   xi

by traits of language and expression of the text or responds to issues of a systematic character pervading the documents in which the particularities of detailed exegesis figure. Such debates, which yield interesting results for the contemporary hermeneutics of Scripture, do not greatly advance our systematic knowledge of the way in which the sages and theologians received Scripture and responded to it. That knowledge depends upon comprehensive surveys of details and the categorization of the details. These desiderata await realization. We cannot now on the basis of a full corpus of data define the range of concerns that drew sages and theologians to Scripture: what they were likely to ask Scripture to reveal, to demonstrate, to elucidate.

To find out we need to collect and classify the corpus of comments on specific verses of Scripture embedded in the writings of the ancient rabbis and theologians. When we have accomplished the work of hunting and gathering the data and inductively ordering it by its interior categories, we shall have established solid foundations for generalization. Then we may say what the sages and theologians proposed to accomplish in their engagement with Scripture. We may begin to outline the authority of Scripture as that authority imposed structure and order upon the sages' and the theologians' systems: for what was Scripture likely to be interrogated, and what were the issues important in late antiquity on which Scripture was not invited to testify. To answer these questions of large-scale characterization and generalization requires a kind of work of collecting and arranging facts that until now has not been done — a reference book on Rabbinic readings of Israelite prophecy.

III

My ambition here is modest. This is a source book produced by grunt work, just a collection and classification of facts meant to provide documentation for the future study of how one particular kind of ancient Israelite Scripture, the prophetic books, found a place in the new language community formed by the Rabbinic sages and documented in their canon from the Mishnah, ca. 200 C.E., through the Talmud of Babylonia, a.k.a., the Bavli, ca. 600 C.E. I have collected from my translations and arranged in sequence document by document the references to the principal prophets set forth in the Rabbinic writings of late antiquity. In the companion studies I classify the uses of prophecy undertaken by the rabbis: the evidences of the movement from language to language, world view to world view. The present collection carries forward *Jeremiah in Talmud and Midrash* (Lanham, 2006: University Press of America. Studies in Judaism series), and its companion *Rabbi Jeremiah*.

The sources and reference system derive from my translations of the canon of formative Judaism. In those translations I consulted prior versions of the same documents. These derive from the British translations published by Soncino Press,

London. Where these are used, I cite the name of the translator and the page in the Soncino translation where the work appears. The reference system I have devised signals the sentence, paragraph, completed unit of thought, plus the document and its conventional divisions, e.g., chapter and subchapter. The use of Aramaic type faces signals Aramaic, plain type, Hebrew, and bold face type, the citation of the Mishnah or the Tosefta by a later document.

The Mishnah. A New Translation. New Haven and London, 1987: Yale University Press. *Choice* Outstanding Academic Book List, 1989. Second printing: 1990. Paperbound edition: 1991. CD Rom edition: Logos, 1996. CD Rom/ Web edition: OakTree Software, Inc. Altamonte Springs, FL.

Editor: *The Law of Agriculture in the Mishnah and the Tosefta.* Leiden, 2005: E. J. Brill.

    I.   *A History of the Mishnaic Law of Agriculture. Berakhot, Peah.*
    II.   *Demai, Kilayim., Shebiit*
    III.   *Terumot, Maaserot, Maaser Sheni, Hallah, Orlah, Bikkurim*

The Tosefta. Translated from the Hebrew. N.Y., 1977-1980: Ktav. II-VI.

    I.   Editor: *The Tosefta. Translated from the Hebrew. I. The First Division Zeraim.* N.Y., 1985: Ktav.
    II.   *The Tosefta. Translated from the Hebrew. The Second Division. Moed.* Second printing: Atlanta, 1999: Scholars Press for USF Academic Commentary Series.
    III.   *The Tosefta. Translated from the Hebrew. The Third Division. Nashim.* Second printing: Atlanta, 1999: Scholars Press for USF Academic Commentary Series.
    IV.   *The Tosefta. Translated from the Hebrew. The Fourth Division. Neziqin.* Second printing: Atlanta, 1999: Scholars Press for USF Academic Commentary Series.
    V.   *The Tosefta. Translated from the Hebrew. The Fifth Division. Qodoshim.* Second printing: Atlanta, 1997: Scholars Press for USF Academic Commentary Series.
    VI.   *The Tosefta. Translated from the Hebrew. The Sixth Division. Tohorot.* Second printing: Atlanta, 1990: Scholars Press for *South Florida Studies in the History of Judaism.* With a new preface.

Reprint: *The Tosefta in English.* I. *Zeraim, Moed, and Nashim.* Peabody, 2003: Hendrickson Publications. With a new introduction.

Preface

Reprint: *The Tosefta in English.* II. *Neziqin, Qodoshim, and Toharot.* Peabody, 2003: Hendrickson Publications.

The Talmud of Babylonia. An Academic Commentary. Atlanta. 1994-1996, 1999: Scholars Press for *USF Academic Commentary Series.* Now: Lanham, MD. University Press of America

I.	*Bavli Tractate Berakhot*
II.A	*Bavli Tractate Shabbat. Chapters One through Twelve*
II.B	*Bavli Tractate Shabbat. Chapters Thirteen through Twenty-Four*
III.A	*Bavli Tractate Erubin. Chapters One through Five*
III.B	*Bavli Tractate Erubin. Chapters Six through Eleven*
IV.A	*Bavli Tractate Pesahim. Chapters One through Seven.*
IV.B	*Bavli Tractate Pesahim. Chapters Eight through Eleven.*
V.	*Bavli Tractate Yoma*
VI.	*Bavli Tractate Sukkah*
VII.	*Bavli Tractate Besah*
VIII.	*Bavli Tractate Rosh Hashanah*
IX.	*Bavli Tractate Taanit* [1999]
X.	*Bavli Tractate Megillah*
XI.	*Bavli Tractate Moed Qatan*
XII.	*Bavli Tractate Hagigah*
XIII.A	*Bavli Tractate Yebamot. Chapters One through Eight*
XIII.B	*Bavli Tractate Yebamot. Chapters Nine through Seventeen*
XIV.A	*Bavli Tractate Ketubot. Chapters One through Six*
XIV.B	*Bavli Tractate Ketubot. Chapters Seven through Fourteen*
XV.	*Bavli Tractate Nedarim*
XVI.	*Bavli Tractate Nazir* [1999]
XVII.	*Bavli Tractate Sotah*
XVIII.	*Bavli Tractate Gittin*
XIX.	*Bavli Tractate Qiddushin*
XX.	*Bavli Tractate Baba Qamma*
XXI.A	*Bavli Tractate Baba Mesia. Chapters One through Six*
XXI.B	*Bavli Tractate Baba Mesia. Chapters Seven through Eleven*
XXII.A	*Bavli Tractate Baba Batra. Chapters One through Six*
XXII.B	*Bavli Tractate Baba Batra. Chapters Seven through Eleven*
XXIII.A	*Bavli Tractate Sanhedrin. Chapters One through Seven*
XXIII.B	*Bavli Tractate Sanhedrin. Chapters Eight through Twelve*
XXIV.	*Bavli Tractate Makkot*
XXV.	*Bavli Tractate Abodah Zarah*
XXVI.	*Bavli Tractate Horayot*
XXVII.	*Bavli Tractate Shebuot*

XXVIII.A *Bavli Tractate Zebahim. Chapters One through Seven*
XXVIII.B *Bavli Tractate Zebahim. Chapters Eight through Fifteen*
XXIX.A *Bavli Tractate Menahot. Chapters One through Six*
XXIX.B *Bavli Tractate Menahot. Chapters Seven through Fourteen*
XXX.   *Bavli Tractate Hullin*
XXXI.   *Bavli Tractate Bekhorot*
XXXII.   *Bavli Tractate Arakhin*
XXXIII   *Bavli Tractate Temurah*
XXXIV.   *Bavli Tractate Keritot*
XXXV.   *Bavli Tractate Meilah and Tamid*
XXXVI.   *Bavli Tractate Niddah*

The *Babylonian Talmud. Translation and Commentary*. Peabody, 2005: Hendrickson Publishing Co. Second printing of *The Talmud of Babylonia. An Academic Commentary*.

    i.   *Berakhot*
    ii.   *Shabbat*
    iii.   *Erubin*
    iv.   *Pesahim*
    v.   *Yoma-Sukkah*
    vi.   *Taanit-Megillah-Moed Qatan-Hagigah*
    vii.   *Besah-Rosh Hashanah*
    viii. *Yebamot*
    ix.   *Ketubot*
    x.   *Nedarim-Nazir*
    xi.   *Sotah-Gittin*
    xii.   *Qiddushin*
    xiii. *Baba Qamma*
    xiv.   *Baba Mesia*
    xv.   *Baba Batra*
    xvi.   *Sanhedrin*
    xvii. *Makkot-Abodah Zarah-Horayot*
    xviii. *Shebuot-Zebahim*
    xix.   *Menahot*
    xx.   *Hullin*
    xxi.   *Bekhorot-Arakhin-Temurah*
    xxii. *Keritot-Meilah-Tamid-Niddah*

The Talmud of Babylonia. A Complete Outline. Atlanta, 1995-6: Scholars Press for *USF Academic Commentary Series*. Now: Lanham, MD. University Press of America

Preface

I.A Tractate Berakhot and the Division of Appointed Times. Berakhot, Shabbat, and Erubin.
I.B Tractate Berakhot and the Division of Appointed Times. Pesahim through Hagigah.
II.A. The Division of Women. Yebamot through Ketubot
II.B. The Division of Women. Nedarim through Qiddushin
III.A The Division of Damages. Baba Qamma through Baba Batra
III.B The Division of Damages. Sanhedrin through Horayot
IV.A The Division of Holy Things and Tractate Niddah. Zebahim through Hullin
IV.B The Division of Holy Things and Tractate Niddah. Bekhorot through Niddah

The Talmud of the Land of Israel. An Academic Commentary to the Second, Third, and Fourth Divisions. Atlanta, 1998-1999: Scholars Press for *USF Academic Commentary Series*. Now: Lanham, MD. University Press of America.

I. Yerushalmi Tractate Berakhot
II.A Yerushalmi Tractate Shabbat. Chapters One through Ten
II.B Yerushalmi Tractate Shabbat. Chapters Eleven through Twenty-Four. And the Structure of Yerushalmi Shabbat
III. Yerushalmi Tractate Erubin
IV. Yerushalmi Tractate Yoma
V.A Yerushalmi Tractate Pesahim. Chapters One through Six.
V.B Yerushalmi Tractate Pesahim. Chapters Seven through Ten. And the Structure of Yerushalmi Pesahim
VI. Yerushalmi Tractate Sukkah
VII. Yerushalmi Tractate Besah
VIII. Yerushalmi Tractate Taanit
IX. Yerushalmi Tractate Megillah
X. Yerushalmi Tractate Rosh Hashanah
XI. Yerushalmi Tractate Hagigah
XII. Yerushalmi Tractate Moed Qatan
XIII.A Yerushalmi Tractate Yebamot. Chapters One through Ten
XIII.B Yerushalmi Tractate Yebamot. Chapters Eleven through Seventeen. And the Structure of Yerushalmi Yebamot
XIV. Yerushalmi Tractate Ketubot
XV. Yerushalmi Tractate Nedarim
XVI. Yerushalmi Tractate Nazir
XVII. Yerushalmi Tractate Gittin
XVIII. Yerushalmi Tractate Qiddushin

XIX. *Yerushalmi Tractate Sotah*
XX. *Yerushalmi Tractate Baba Qamma*
XXI. *Yerushalmi Tractate Baba Mesia*
XXII. *Yerushalmi Tractate Baba Batra*
XXIII. *Yerushalmi Tractate Sanhedrin*
XXIV. *Yerushalmi Tractate Makkot*
XXV. *Yerushalmi Tractate Shebuot*
XXVI. *Yerushalmi Tractate Abodah Zarah*
XXVII. *Yerushalmi Tractate Horayot*
XXVIII. *Yerushalmi Tractate Niddah*

The Talmud of The Land of Israel. An Outline of the Second, Third, and Fourth Divisions. Atlanta, 1995-6: Scholars Press for USF Academic Commentary Series. Now: Lanham, MD. University Press of America

    I.A   *Tractate Berakhot and the Division of Appointed Times. Berakhot and Shabbat*
    I.B   *Tractate Berakhot and the Division of Appointed Times. Erubin, Yoma, and Besah*
    I.C   *Tractate Berakhot and the Division of Appointed Times. Pesahim and Sukkah*
    I.D   *Tractate Berakhot and the Division of Appointed Times. Taanit, Megillah, Rosh Hashanah, Hagigah, and Moed Qatan*
    II.A *The Division of Women. Yebamot to Nedarim*
    II.B *The Division of Women. Nazir to Sotah*
    III.A *The Division of Damages and Tractate Niddah. Baba Qamma, Baba Mesia, Baba Batra, Horayot, and Niddah*
    III.B *The Division of Damages and Tractate Niddah. Sanhedrin, Makkot, Shebuot, and Abodah Zarah*

The Two Talmuds Compared. Atlanta, 1995-6: Scholars Press for USF Academic Commentary Series. *The Talmud of the Land of Israel. An Academic Commentary to the Second, Third, and Fourth Divisions.* Atlanta, 1998-1999: Scholars Press for *USF Academic Commentary Series.* Now: Lanham, MD. University Press of America.

    I.A   *Tractate Berakhot and the Division of Appointed Times in the Talmud of the Land of Israel and the Talmud of Babylonia. Yerushalmi Tractate Berakhot*
    I.B   *Tractate Berakhot and the Division of Appointed Times in the Talmud of the Land of Israel and the Talmud of Babylonia. Tractate Shabbat.*

I.C   *Tractate Berakhot and the Division of Appointed Times in the Talmud of the Land of Israel and the Talmud of Babylonia. Tractate Erubin*

I.D   *Tractate Berakhot and the Division of Appointed Times in the Talmud of the Land of Israel and the Talmud of Babylonia. Tractates Yoma and Sukkah*

I.E   *Tractate Berakhot and the Division of Appointed Times in the Talmud of the Land of Israel and the Talmud of Babylonia. Tractate Pesahim*

I.F   *Tractate Berakhot and the Division of Appointed Times in the Talmud of the Land of Israel and the Talmud of Babylonia. Tractates Besah, Taanit, and Megillah*

I.G   *Tractate Berakhot and the Division of Appointed Times in the Talmud of the Land of Israel and the Talmud of Babylonia. Tractates Rosh Hashanah, Hagigah, and Moed Qatan*

II.A   *The Division of Women in the Talmud of the Land of Israel and the Talmud of Babylonia. Tractates Yebamot and Ketubot.*

II.B   *The Division of Women in the Talmud of the Land of Israel and the Talmud of Babylonia. Tractates Nedarim, Nazir, and Sotah.*

II.C   *The Division of Women in the Talmud of the Land of Israel and the Talmud of Babylonia. Tractates Qiddushin and Gittin.*

III.A   *The Division of Damages and Tractate Niddah in the Talmud of the Land of Israel and the Talmud of Babylonia. Tractates Baba Qamma and Baba Mesia*

III.B   *The Division of Damages and Tractate Niddah in the Talmud of the Land of Israel and the Talmud of Babylonia. Baba Batra and Niddah.*

III.C   *The Division of Damages and Tractate Niddah. Sanhedrin and Makkot.*

III.D   *The Division of Damages and Tractate Niddah. Shebuot, Abodah Zarah, and Horayot.*

The Components of the Rabbinic Documents: From the Whole to the Parts. I. *Sifra.* Atlanta, 1997: Scholars Press for USF Academic Commentary Series.

Part i.   *Introduction. And Parts One through Three, Chapters One through Ninety-Eight*

Part ii.   *Parts Four through Nine. Chapters Ninety-Nine through One Hundred Ninety-Four*

Part iii. *Parts Ten through Thirteen. Chapters One Hundred Ninety-Five through Two Hundred Seventy-Seven*

Part iv. *A Topical and Methodical Outline of Sifra*

The Components of the Rabbinic Documents: From the Whole to the Parts. II. *Esther Rabbah I.* Atlanta, 1997: Scholars Press for USF Academic Commentary Series.

The Components of the Rabbinic Documents: From the Whole to the Parts. III. *Ruth Rabbah.* Atlanta, 1997: Scholars Press for USF Academic Commentary Series.

The Components of the Rabbinic Documents: From the Whole to the Parts. IV. *Lamentations Rabbati.* Atlanta, 1997: Scholars Press for USF Academic Commentary Series.

The Components of the Rabbinic Documents: From the Whole to the Parts. V. *Song of Songs Rabbah.* Atlanta, 1997: Scholars Press for USF Academic Commentary Series.

    Part i. *Introduction. And Parashiyyot One through Four*
    Part ii. *Parashiyyot Five through Eight. And a Topical and Methodical Outline of Song of Songs Rabbah*

The Components of the Rabbinic Documents: From the Whole to the Parts. VI. *The Fathers Attributed to Rabbi Nathan.* Atlanta, 1997: Scholars Press for USF Academic Commentary Series.

The Components of the Rabbinic Documents: From the Whole to the Parts. VII. *Sifré to Deuteronomy.* Atlanta, 1997: Scholars Press for USF Academic Commentary Series.

    Part i. *Introduction. And Parts One through Four*
    Part ii. *Parts Five through Ten*
    Part iii. *A Topical and Methodical Outline of Sifré to Deuteronomy*

The Components of the Rabbinic Documents: From the Whole to the Parts. VIII. *Mekhilta Attributed to R. Ishmael.* Atlanta, 1997: Scholars Press for USF Academic Commentary Series

    Part i. *Introduction. Pisha, Beshallah and Shirata*
    Part ii *Vayassa, Amalek, Bahodesh, Neziqin, Kaspa and Shabbata*
    Part iii. *A Topical and Methodical Outline of Mekhilta Attributed to R. Ishmael.*

Preface

The Components of the Rabbinic Documents: From the Whole to the Parts. IX. Atlanta, 1998: Scholars Press for USF Academic Commentary Series. Now: Lanham, University Press of America.

    Part i. *Introduction. Genesis Rabbah Chapters One through Twenty-One*
    Part ii. *Genesis Rabbah Chapters Twenty-Two through Forty-Eight*
    Part iii. *Genesis Rabbah Chapters Forty-Nine through Seventy-Three*
    Part iv. *Genesis Rabbah Chapters Seventy-Four through One Hundred*
    Part v. *A Topical and Methodical Outline of Genesis Rabbah. Bereshit through Vaere, Chapters One through Fifty-Seven*
    Part vi. *A Topical and Methodical Outline of Genesis Rabbah. Hayye Sarah through Miqqes. Chapters Fifty-Eight through One Hundred*

The Components of the Rabbinic Documents: From the Whole to the Parts. X. *Leviticus Rabbah.* Atlanta, 1998: Scholars Press for USF Academic Commentary Series.

    Part i. *Introduction. Leviticus Rabbah Parashiyyot One through Seventeen*
    Part ii. *Leviticus Rabbah Parashiyyot Eighteen through Thirty-Seven*
    Part iii. *Leviticus Rabbah. A Topical and Methodical Outline*

The Components of the Rabbinic Documents: From the Whole to the Parts. XI. *Pesiqta deRab Kahana.* Atlanta, 1998: Scholars Press for USF Academic Commentary Series.

    Part i. *Introduction. Pesiqta deRab Kahana Pisqaot One through Eleven*
    Part ii. *Pesiqta deRab Kahana Pisqaot Twelve through Twenty-Eight*
    Part iii. *Pesiqta deRab Kahana. A Topical and Methodical Outline*

The Components of the Rabbinic Documents: From the Whole to the Parts. XII. *Sifré to Numbers.* Atlanta, 1998: Scholars Press for USF Academic Commentary Series.

    Part i. *Introduction. Pisqaot One through Eighty-Four*
    Part ii *Pisqaot Eighty-Five through One Hundred Twenty-Two*
    Part iii *Pisqaot One Hundred Twenty-Three through One Hundred Sixty-One*
    Part iv *Sifré to Numbers. A Topical and Methodical Outline*

The Rabbinic Midrash. Peabody, 2006: Hendrickson Publishing Co. Second printing, in twelve volumes, of *The Components of the Rabbinic Documents: From the Whole to the Parts.*

In addition to *Jeremiah in Talmud and Midrash* (Lanham, 2006: University Press of America), which is already in print, and the present anthology of Amos, I plan to compose sourcebooks for all of the literary prophets, as follows:

Hosea in Talmud and Midrash. A Source Book. Lanham: University Press of America STUDIES IN JUDAISM SERIES

Isaiah in Talmud and Midrash. A Source Book. Lanham: University Press of America STUDIES IN JUDAISM SERIES

Ezekiel in Talmud and Midrash. A Source Book. Lanham: University Press of America STUDIES IN JUDAISM SERIES

Joel in Talmud and Midrash. A Source Book. Lanham: University Press of America STUDIES IN JUDAISM SERIES

Obadiah in Talmud and Midrash. A Source Book. Lanham: University Press of America STUDIES IN JUDAISM SERIES

Jonah in Talmud and Midrash. A Source Book. Lanham: University Press of America STUDIES IN JUDAISM SERIES

Micah in Talmud and Midrash. A Source Book. Lanham: University Press of America STUDIES IN JUDAISM SERIES

Nahum in Talmud and Midrash. A Source Book. Lanham: University Press of America STUDIES IN JUDAISM SERIES

Habakkuk in Talmud and Midrash. A Source Book. Lanham: University Press of America STUDIES IN JUDAISM SERIES

Zephaniah in Talmud and Midrash. A Source Book. Lanham: University Press of America STUDIES IN JUDAISM SERIES

Haggai in Talmud and Midrash. A Source Book. Lanham: University Press of America STUDIES IN JUDAISM SERIES

Zechariah in Talmud and Midrash. A Source Book. Lanham: University Press of America STUDIES IN JUDAISM SERIES

Malachi in Talmud and Midrash. A Source Book. Lanham: University Press of America STUDIES IN JUDAISM SERIES

I am pleased to acknowledge the advice in planning this project of colleagues in biblical studies, in particular Richard E. Friedman, University of Georgia; Alan Cooper, The Jewish Theological Seminary of America; Bernard Levinson, University of Minnesota; and Jon Levenson, Harvard University. Their advice is always valuable. For planning the project as a whole I further consulted William Scott Green, University of Rochester, Herbert Basser, Queen's University, and Bruce D. Chilton, Bard College.

Jacob Neusner
Research Professor of Theology
Senior Fellow, Institute of Advanced Theology
Bard College
Annandale-on-Hudson, New York 12504 5000

ENDNOTES

[1] Nicholas Ostler, *Empires of the Word. A Language History of the World* (N.Y. 2005: HarperCollins), p. 13.

1

Amos in the Mishnah, Tractate Abot and the Tosefta

MISHNAH

Mishnah Taanit 3:3
- A. And so too: A town on which rain did not fall,
- B. as it is said, "And I caused it to rain upon one city and caused it not to rain upon another city, one piece was rained upon and the piece on which it rained did not wither" (Amos 4:7)
- C. that town declares a fast day and sounds the shofar
- D. And all its neighbors fast but do not sound the shofar
- E. R. Aqiba says, "They sound the shofar but do not fast."

Amos supplies a case to illustrate the law. God is responsible for rain in one place, not another, and hence the Shofar is sounded in response.

Mishnah Yadayim 4:4
- A. On that day:
- B. Judah an Ammonite proselyte came and stood before them in the *bet hammidrash*.
- C. He said to them, "Am I allowed to enter the congregation?"
- D. Rabban Gamaliel said to him, "You are forbidden [to enter the congregation],"
- E. R. Joshua said to him, "You are permitted."
- F. Rabban Gamaliel said to him, "Scripture says, 'An Ammonite or a Moabite shall not enter into the assembly of the Lord, even to the tenth generation' (Dt. 23:4)."
- G. R. Joshua said to him, "And are there Ammonites and Moabites in this place?

H. "Already has Sennacherib, king of Assyria, come up and mixed up all the nations.
I. "As it is said, 'I have removed the bounds of the peoples and have robbed their treasures and have brought down as a valiant man them that sit on thrones' (Is. 10:13)."
J. Rabban Gamaliel said to him, "Scripture says, 'But afterward I will bring again the captivity of the children of Ammon' (Jer. 49:6). And indeed they have returned."
K. R. Joshua said to him, "Scripture says, 'And I will return the captivity of my people Israel and Judah, says the Lord' (Amos 9:14). And as yet they have not returned."
L. And they permitted him to enter into the congregation.

Amos provides a fact for the Halakhic ruling.

TRACTATE ABOT

I find no reference to Amos in tractate Abot.

TOSEFTA

Tosefta Berakhot 2:17
A. One should not enter filthy alleyways [soiled with excrement] and recite the Shema'.
B. Furthermore, even if one entered [the alleyway) while he was reciting [the shema'], behold, this one must interrupt [his recitation] until he leaves the vicinity of that place, and [then] he may recite.

Tosefta Berakhot 2:18
A. One should not stand to pray [i.e., recite the Prayer] if he needs to relieve himself,
B. as Scripture states, "Prepare to meet your God, O Israel" (Amos 4:12).

Amos supplies a proof-text that one should prepare for prayer by doing other needs that might disrupt his piety.

Tosefta Eduyyot 1:1
A. When sages came together in the vineyard at Yabneh, they said, "The time is coming at which a person will go looking for a teaching of Torah and will not find it,
B. "a teaching of scribes and will not find it,
C. "since it is said, 'Behold, the days are coming, says the Lord Cod, when I will send a famine on the land; not a famine of bread, nor a thirst for water, but of hearing the words of the Lord. They shall wander from sea to sea and from north to east, they shall run to and fro, to seek the word of the Lord, but they shall not find it' (Amos 8:12).

D. "The word of the Lord" refers to prophecy.
   E. "The word of the Lord" refers to [knowledge of] the end.
   F. "The word of the Lord" means that not one word of the Torah is the same as another word of the Torah.
   G. They said, "Let us begin from Hillel and from Shammai."

Amos's prophecy is amplified and drawn into the framework of Rabbinic Torah. The word of the Lord in Amos refers not only to prophecy but also knowledge o the end-time and knowledge of the Torah.

Tosefta Kippurim 4:13
   A. R. Yosé says, "[If] a man sins two or three times, they forgive him. [But on the] fourth, they do not forgive him,
   B. "as it says, 'Forgiving iniquity, transgression, and sin, but he will by no means clear the guilty' (Ex. 34:7).
   C. "Up to this point he clears [him]. From this point forward he will not clear [him],
   D. "since it says, 'For three transgressions of Israel — but for four, I will not turn away the punishment' (Amos 2:6).
   E. "And it says, 'He will deliver his soul from going into the piTosefta All these things does God do two or three times for a man' (Job 33:28-29).
   F. "And it says, 'Withdraw your foot from your neighbor's house lest he be weary of you' (Prov. 25:16)."

Amos places limits on the divine forgiveness, in line with Ex. 34:7.

Tosefta Shabbat 7:3
   A. He who says, "Dani," "Dano," — lo, this is one of "the ways of the Amorites."
   B. R. Judah says, "This is because of the idol, Dan,'
   C. "since it says, 'As thy god lives, O Dan,' and, 'As the way of Beersheba lives' (Amos 8:17)."

Amos supplies data for interpreting the law.

Tosefta Shabbat 7:24
   A. R. Nehorai says, "You have no city more considerate than the Sodomites.
   B. "And so we find that Lot went through every place and found no place so considerate as Sodom,
   C. "since it says, 'And Abram dwelt in the land of Canaan' (Gen. 13:12)."
7:25 A. And Rabban Gamaliel says, "You have no people which is more considerate than the Amorites.

>   B. "And so we find that they believed in the Omnipresent and were exiled to Africa.
>   C. "The Omnipresent gave them a land as beautiful as their original land.
>   D. "'And the land of Israel was called by their name' (Amos 2:10)."

Amos contributes a fact in support of Gamaliel's view of the Amorites.

Tosefta Yadayim 2:16

>   A. Said R. Yosé the Damascene, "I was with the former elders going thereafter] from Yavneh to Lud, and I came and found R. Eliezer.
>   B. "For he was sitting in the stall of bakers in Lud.
>   C. "He said to me, 'What new thing was there in the *bet hammidrash*?'
>   D. "I said to him, 'Rabbi, We are your disciples and drink from your water.'
>   E. "He said to me, 'Even so — what new thing [did you hear]?'
>   F. "I reported to him the laws and responsa and the vote.
>   G. "And when I came to this matter, his eyes filled with tears. He said "'The secret of the Lord is with those that fear him' (Ps. 125:14). And it says, 'Surely the Lord God does nothing without revealing his secret to his servants the prophets' (Amos 3:7).
>   H. "Go and say to them, 'Do not be anxious about your vote. I have a tradition from Rabban Yohanan b. Zakkai, which he received from the pairs, and the pairs from the prophets, and the prophets from Moses, a law [revealed] to Moses at Sinai:
>   "'They tithe the tithe of the poor man in the Sabbatical year.'"

Amos speaks of prophets and the Rabbinic passage assumes he means sages. Eliezer places Yohanan ben Zakkai in the chain of tradition that extends backward to the prophets and to Moses, explicitly so in the reference to "his servants the prophets" in the setting of Yohanan.

2

Amos in Sifra, the Two Sifrés and the Mekhilta Attributed to R. Ishmael

SIFRA

I find no reference to Amos.

SIFRÉ TO NUMBERS

Sifré to Numbers LXVII:I
1. A. "And they kept the Passover in the first month, on the fourteenth day of the month, [in the evening, in the wilderness of Sinai; according to all that the Lord commanded Moses, so the people of Israel did]" (Num. 9:1-14):
   B. Scripture records the disgrace of Israel, for they observed only this Passover alone.
   C. And so Scripture states, "Did you even offer to me [plural] sacrifices and meal-offerings in the wilderness" (Amos 5:25) [with the answer, no, only that one].
   D. R. Simeon b. Yohai says, "Since Israel did not make such offerings, then who made the offerings? It was only the tribe of Levi, as it is said, '*They* shall put incense before you and whole burnt offering upon your altar' (Deut. 33:10).
   E. "And Scripture says, 'And Moses stood at the gate of the camp and said, "Whoever is for the Lord, come to me"' (Ex. 33:26). While Israel served idolatry, the tribe of Levi did not serve idolatry, as it is said, 'For they observed your word and kept your covenant' (Deut. 33:9).
   F. "And Scripture further states, 'Though all the people who came out had been circumcised, yet all the people that were born on the way in the wilderness after they had come out of Egypt had not been circumcised' (Joshua 5:5), indicating that the Israelites had

not practiced circumcision, but who did? It was the tribe of Levi, as it is said, 'For they observed your word and kept your covenant [of circumcision]' (Deut. 33:9)."

Amos condemns the Israelites for not offering sacrifices and meal-offerings in the wilderness. But the Levites did make the offerings, and they did so without serving idolatry. This turns Amos's statement, "Di you even offer to me sacrifices…," from a rejection of sacrifices to an accusation of having failed to present them. The issue now is shifted to which Israelites failed, and it was the Israelites not the Levites. Any hint of rejection of Temple offerings is removed.

Sifré to Numbers CXIX:III

3. A. R. Eleazar Haqqappar says, "How do you know that the Holy One, blessed be he, showed to Jacob our father the house of the sanctuary in all its beauty and the offerings being presented, the priests serving, and the Presence of God rising up? As it is said, 'And he dreamed, and behold, a ladder was set on the ground, with its head reaching the heaven, and lo, angels of God were going up and coming down on it' (Gen. 28:12). There is no such thing as a dream without a proper interpretation, which is, in this case, s follows:
   B. "'And he dreamed, and behold, a ladder was set on the ground:' this refers to the house of the sanctuary.
   C. "'with its head reaching the heaven:' this refers to the offerings being presented, the odor of which rises to heaven.
   D. "'and lo, angels of God were going up and coming down on it:' this refers to the priests in their acts of service, who go up and come down on the ramp around the altar.
   E. "And lo, the Lord is standing on it, 'and I saw the Lord standing at the altar' (Amos 9:1)."

Once more the offerings are affirmed. The Lord is seen by Amos to be standing at the altar. Any hint that sacrifice is null is dismissed.

"Miriam and Aaron spoke against Moses [because of the Kushite woman whom he had married, for he had married a Kushite woman; and they said, 'Has the Lord indeed spoken only through Moses? Has he not spoken through us also?' And the Lord heard it. Now the man Moses was very meek, more than all men that were on the face of the earth. And suddenly the Lord said to Moses and to Aaron and Miriam, 'Come out, you three, to the tent of meeting.' And the three of them came out. And the Lord came down in a pillar of cloud and stood at the door of the tent and called Aaron and Miriam; and they both came forward. And he said, 'Hear my words, if there is a prophet among you, I the Lord make myself known to him in a vision, I speak with him in a dream. Not so with my servant Moses; he is entrusted with all my house. With him I speak mouth to mouth, clearly, and not in dark speech, and he beholds the form of the Lord. Why then were you not afraid to speak against my servant Moses?' And the anger of the Lord was kindled against them, and he departed; and when the cloud removed from over the tent, behold, Miriam was leprous, as

2. Amos in Sifra...

white as snow. And Aaron turned towards Miriam, and behold, she was leprous. And Aaron said to Moses, 'Oh my lord, do not punish us, because we have done foolishly and have sinned. Let her not be as one dead, of whom the flesh is half consumed, when he comes out of his mother's womb.' And Moses cried to the Lord, 'Heal her, O God, I beseech you.' But the Lord said to Moses, 'If her father had but spit in her face, should she not be shamed seven days? Let he be shut up outside the camp seven days, and after that she may be brought in again.' So Miriam was shut up outside the camp seven days, and the people did not set out on the march till Miriam was brought in again. And after that the people set out from Hazeroth and encamped in the wilderness of Paran]" (Num. 12:1-16):

Sifré to Numbers XCIX:III

2. A. "...because of the Kushite woman:"
   B. Was she a Kushite [Ethiopian]? Was she not a Midianite? For it is said, "And the priest of Midian had seven daughters" (Ex., 2:16).
   C. Why then does Scripture refer to her as a Kushite?
   D. The meaning is that just as a Kushite has skin different from others, so Zipporah was different from others in beauty, more beautiful than all other women.
   E. Along these same lines: "A *shiggaon* of David, which he sang to the Lord concerning the words of Cush the Benjaminite" (Ps. 7:1).
   F. Now was he a Kushite? The meaning is that just as a Kushite has skin different from others, so Saul was distinctive in his appearance, as it is said, "From his shoulders and upward he was taller than the entire people" (1 Sam. 9:2).
   G. Along these same lines: "Are you not like the sons of the Kushites to me, O children of Israel" (Amos 9:7).
   H. Now were they Kushites? The meaning is that just as a Kushite has skin different from others, so the Israelites are distinguished in the doing of religious duties, more so than all the nations of the world.
   I. Along these same lines: "And a servant of the king, a Kushite eunuch, heard..." (Jer. 38:7).
   J. Now was he a Kushite? The meaning is that just as a Kushite has skin different from others, so Baruch b. Neriah was distinguished in his deeds among all the members of the king's establishment.

Israel is compared to the Kushites, when Amos says that the Israelites are to God just like the Kushites. What they have in common is that they are distinguished among the nations of the world, specifically by carrying out religious imperatives.

Sifré to Deuteronomy

Sifré to Deuteronomy I:I

1. A. "These are the words that Moses spoke to all Israel in Transjordan, in the wilderness, that is to say in the Arabah, opposite Suph, between Paran on the one side and Tophel, Laban, Hazeroth, and Dizahab, on the other" (Dt. 1:1):

B. ["These are the words that Moses spoke" (Dt. 1:1):] Did Moses prophesy only these alone? Did he not write the entire Torah?
C. For it is said, "And Moses wrote this Torah" (Dt. 31:9).
D. Why then does Scripture say, "These are the words that Moses spoke" (Dt. 1:1)?
E. It teaches that [when Scripture speaks of the words that one spoke, it refers in particular to] the words of admonition.
F. So it is said [by Moses], "But Jeshurun waxed fat and kicked" (Dt. 32:15).

2. A. So too you may point to the following:
B. "The words of Amos, who was among the herdsman of Tekoa, which he saw concerning Israel in the days of Uzziah, king of Judah, and in the days of Jeroboam, son of Joash, king of Israel, two years before the earthquake" (Amos 1:1):
C. Did Amos prophesy only concerning these [kings] alone? Did he not prophesy more than any other [prophet]?
D. Why then does Scripture say, "These are the words of Amos, [who was among the herdsman of Tekoa, which he saw concerning Israel in the days of Uzziah, king of Judah, and in the days of Jeroboam, son of Joash, king of Israel, two years before the earthquake]" (Amos 1:1).
E. It teaches that [when Scripture speaks of the words that one spoke, it refers in particular to] the words of admonition.
F. And how do we know that they were words of admonition?
G. As it is said, "Hear this word, you cows of Bashan, who are in the mountain of Samaria, who oppress the poor, crush the needy, and say to their husbands, 'Bring, that we may feast'" (Amos 4:1).
H. ["And say to their husbands, 'Bring, that we may feast'"] speaks of their courts.

Amos provides an example of the proposition that when Scripture speaks of the words that one spoke it refers to words of admonition.

"...you have begun [to show your servant the first works of your greatness and your mighty hand, you whose deeds and acts of might no god in heaven or on earth can equal! Let me, I pray, cross over and see the good land on the other side of the Jordan, that good hill country, and the Lebanon.' But the Lord was wrathful with me on your account and would not listen to me. The Lord said to me, 'Enough, never speak to me of this matter again! Go up to the summit of Pisgah and gaze about, to the west, the north, the south, and the east. Look at it well, for you shall not go across yonder Jordan. Give Joshua his instructions and imbue him with strength and courage, for he shall go across at the head of this people, and he shall allot to them the land that you may only see.' Meanwhile we stayed on in the valley near Beth-peor]" (Dt. 4:23-29):

Sifré to Deuteronomy XXVII:III

1. A. "...to show your servant the first works of your greatness":
B. There are [1] those who called themselves servants, and the Holy

2. Amos in Sifra...

One, blessed be He, called them servants, and [2] there are those who called themselves servants, and the Holy One, blessed be He, did not call them servants, and [3] there are those who did not call themselves servants, but the Holy One, blessed be He, called them servants:

C. Abraham called himself a servant: "Do not pass away, I ask, from your servant" (Gen. 18:3), and the Holy One, blessed be He, called him a servant: "For my servant Abraham's sake" (Gen. 26:24).

D. Jacob called himself a servant: "I am not worthy of all the mercies, and of all the truth, which you have shown to your servant" (Gen. 32:11), and God called him a servant: "But you, Israel, my servant" (Is. 41:8).

E. Moses called himself a servant: "To show your servant...," and the Holy One, blessed be He, also called him a servant: "My servant, Moses, is not so" (Num. 12:7).

F. David called himself a servant: "I am your servant, the son of your servant-girl" (Ps. 116:16), and the Holy One, blessed be He, also called him a servant: "For I will defend this city to save it for my own sake and for the sake of my servant, David" (12 Kgs. 19:34), "And David my servant shall be their prince for ever" (Ez. 37:25).

G. Isaiah called himself a servant: "And now says the Lord who formed me from the womb to be his servant" (Is. 49:5), and the Holy One, blessed be He, also called him a servant: "Like my servant Isaiah has walked naked and barefoot" (Is. 20:3).

H. Samuel called himself a servant: "Then Samuel said, 'Speak, for your servant is listening'" (1 Sam. 3:10), but the Holy One, blessed be He, did not call him a servant.

I. Samson called himself a servant: "You have given this great deliverance by the hand of your servant" (Judges. 115 18), but the Holy One, blessed be He, did not call him servant.

J. Solomon called himself a servant: "Give your servant, therefore, an understanding heart" (1 Kgs. 3:9), but the Holy One, blessed be He, did not call him servant, but rather made him depend upon his father. David: "For David my servant's sake" (1 Kgs. 11:13).

[3] K. Job did not call himself a servant, but the Holy One, blessed be He, called him a servant: "You have considered my servant Job?" (Job 2:3).

L. Joshua did not call himself a servant, but the Holy One, blessed be He, called him a servant: "Joshua the son of Nun, the servant of the Lord, died" (Josh. 24:29).

M. Caleb did not call himself a servant, but the Holy One, blessed be He, called him a servant: "But my servant, Caleb" (Num. 14:24).

N. Eliakim did not call himself a servant, but the Holy One, blessed be He, called him a servant: "That I will call my servant Eliakim" (Is. 22:20).

O. Zerubbabel did not call himself a servant, but the Holy One, blessed be He, called him a servant: "In that day, says the Lord of hosts, will I take you, O Zerubbabel, my servant, son of Shealtiel, and I will make you as a signet, for I have chosen you, says the Lord of hosts" (Hag. 2:23).

P. Daniel did not call himself a servant, but the Holy One, blessed be He, called him a servant: "O Daniel, servant of the living God" (Dan. 6:21).

Q. Hananiah, Mishael, and Azariah did not call themselves servants, but the Holy One, blessed be He, called them servants: "Shadrach, Meshach, and Abed-nego, you servants of God Most High, come forth and come here" (Dan. 3:26).

R. The former prophets did not call themselves servants, but the Holy One, blessed be He, called them servants: "For the Lord God will do nothing unless he tells his plan to his servants the prophets" (Amos 3:7).

God called the former prophets servants, as proved by Amos's statement.

Sifré to Deuteronomy XLI:II

1. A. "That you may learn them and observe to do them" (Dt. 5:1):
   B. The phrasing of this clause indicates that deed depends on learning, and learning does not depend on deed.
   C. And so we find that a more severe penalty pertains to [neglect of] learning more than to [neglect of doing required] deeds.
   D. For it is said, "Hear the word of the Lord, you children of Israel. For the Lord has a controversy with the inhabitants of the land, because there is no truth nor mercy nor knowledge of God in the land" (Hos. 4:1).
   E. "...there is no truth": truthful words are not said: "Buy the truth and do not sell it [also wisdom, instruction, and understanding]" (Prov. 23:23).
   F. "...nor mercy": merciful words are not said: "The earth, O Lord, is full of your mercy" (Ps. 119:64).
   G. "...nor knowledge of God in the land": knowledgeable words are not said: "My people are destroyed for lack of knowledge [because you have rejected knowledge, I will also reject you, that you shall not be a priest of mine, seeing that you have forgotten the law of your God, I also will forget your children]" (Hos. 4:6).

2. A. "Therefore as stubble devours the tongue of fire and as chaff consumes the flame [so their root shall be as rottenness]" (Is. 5:24):
   B. Is there such a thing as stubble that devours fire?
   C. But "stubble" refers to Esau, that wicked man. For so long as the Israelites give up their hold on their religious duties, he rules over them.

3. A. "Who is the wise man who may understand this? And who is he to whom the mouth of the Lord has spoken, that he may declare it? On that account the land has perished and is laid waste like a

2. Amos in Sifra...

wilderness, so that none passes through? And the Lord says, 'Because they have forsaken my law which I set before them and have not listened to my voice nor walked therein" (Jer. 9:11-12).

4. A. And it says, "Thus says the Lord, 'For three transgressions of Judah, yes, for four, I will not reverse it, because they have rejected the law of the Lord and have not kept his statutes" (Amos 2:4).

5. A. R. Tarfon, R. Aqiba, R. Yosé the Galilean were reclining [at a meal] in the house of Aris in Lydda. This question was presented to them: "What is more important, learning or action?"
   B. Said R. Tarfon, "Action is more important."
   C. R. Aqiba says, "Greater is learning."
   D. All responded, saying, "More important is learning, for learning brings about action."
   E. R. Yosé the Galilean says, "Learning is more important, for the religious duty to learn [and study the Torah] came prior to the religious duty to separate dough-offering by forty years, to separate tithes by fifty-four years [the conquest of the land requiring fourteen], the obligation of the taboo of the years of release by sixty-one years, and prior to the requirement to observe the jubilee years by one hundred and three."

Judah is punished for rejecting the Torah, so Amos.

Sifré to Deuteronomy XLIII:IV

1. A. Another comment concerning the verse, "Take care not to be lured away to serve other gods and bow to them. [For the Lord's anger will flare up against you, and he will shut up the skies so that there be no rain and the ground will not yield its produce; and you will soon perish from the good land that the Lord is assigning to you]" (Dt. 11:13-17):
   B. He said to them, "Take heed that the impulse to do evil not cause you to go astray, and you separate from the Torah.
   C. "For once a person separates from the Torah, he goes and cleaves to idolatry."
   D. For it is said, "They have turned aside quickly out of the way which I commanded them, they have made them a molten calf" (Ex. 32:8).
   E. And further: "If it be the Lord who has stirred you up against me, let him accept an offering, but if it be the children of men, cursed be they before the Lord, for they have driven me out this day that I should not cleave to the inheritance of the Lord, saying, 'Go serve other gods'" (1 Sam. 26:19).
   F. Now can it enter your mind that David, the king, would worship an idol?
   G. But once one ceases to study the words of the Torah, he goes and cleaves to idolatry.

Sifré to Deuteronomy XLIII:VI

1. A. "...to be lured away":

    B.   from the way of life to the way of death.

Sifré to Deuteronomy XLIII:VI

1. A. "...to serve other gods [and bow to them. For the Lord's anger will flare up against you, and he will shut up the skies so that there be no rain and the ground will not yield its produce; and you will soon perish from the good land that the Lord is assigning to you]" (Dt. 11:13-17):
   B. Are they gods at all? Has it not already been stated, "And have cast their gods into the fire; for they were no gods, but the work of men's hands, wood and stone, therefore they have destroyed them" (Is. 37:19).
   C. Why are they called "other gods" then?
   D. For they postpone [using the same letters as the word for "other"] goodness from coming into the world.
5. A. When were they called by his name?
   B. In the time of Enosh, son of Seth. For it is said, "Then men began to call idols by the name of the Lord" (Gen. 4:26).
   C. Then the ocean went and covered a third of the world.
   D. Said to them the Holy One, blessed be He, "You have done a new thing on your own initiative in calling [idols by my name]. So I too shall do a new thing and on my own initiative I shall call [the ocean]."
   E. So it is said, "Who calls for the waters of the sea and pours them out upon the face of the earth, the Lord is his name" (Amos 5:8).

Amos has God punish the Israelites' initiative in calling idols by his name; this he does by doing a new thing and calling the water of the sea and pouring it out over the face of the earth, I assume a reference to the flood in the time of Noah.

Sifré to Deuteronomy XLIII:XIII

1. A. Another matter concerning, "For the Lord's anger will flare up against you, [and he will shut up the skies so that there be no rain and the ground will not yield its produce; and you will soon perish from the good land that the Lord is assigning to you]" (Dt. 11:13-17):
   B. [God speaks,] "Then, after all the sufferings that I shall bring against you, I shall send you into exile."
2. A. Exile is dreadful, since it weighs in the balance against everything else:
   B. "And the Lord rooted them out of their land in anger and in wrath and in great indignation and cast them into another land, as it is this day" (Dt. 29:27).
   C. "And it shall come to pass when they shall say to you, 'Where shall we go,' you then shall say to them, 'Such as are for death, to death, and such as are for the sword, to the sword, and such as are for the famine, to the famine, and such as are for captivity, to

captivity'" (Jer. 15:2).
- D. "Thus says the Lord: 'Your wife shall be a harlot in the city, and your sons and daughter shall fall by the sword, and your land shall be divided by line, and you yourself shall die in an unclean land, and Israel shall surely be led away captive out of his land'" (Amos 7:17).

Amos illustrates the awful character of exile.

Sifré to Deuteronomy XLVII:IV

1. A. Lo, Scripture says, "Yet the number of the children of Israel shall be as the sand of the sea, which cannot be measured or numbered" (Hos. 2:1).
   B. When the Israelites carry out the will of the Omnipresent: "...as the sand of the sea which cannot be measured or numbered."
   C. And if not, "yet the number of the children of Israel shall be."
2. A. And Scripture says, "[One thousand shall flee at the rebuke of one, at the rebuke of five shall you flee,] until you are left as a beacon upon the top of a mountain" (Is. 34 9:17).
   B. "For thus says the Lord God, the city that went forth a thousand shall have a hundred left" (Amos 5:3).

The decline in population comes about because of the failure to do God's will.

Sifré to Deuteronomy XLVIII:V

1. A. Lo, it is stated, "They shall run to and fro to seek the word of the Lord and shall not find it" (Amos 8:12):
   B. Our masters have given permission for disciples to go from village to village and town to town to find out the rule concerning a dead creeping thing that has come into contact with a loaf of bread, specifically, whether it is in the first or the second remove of uncleanness.
2. A. R. Simeon b. Yohai says, "If someone suggests that the Torah might be forgotten in Israel, has it not been said, 'For it shall not be forgotten out of the mouths of their seed' (Dt. 31:21)?
   B. "Rather, [what will happen is this:] 'Mr. X prohibits, Mr. Y permits,' 'Mr. X declares unclean,' Mr. Y declares clean' — but no decisive ruling will be found."

"Seeking the word of the Lord" and not finding it involves the fruitless search for a Halakhic tradition, with special reference to a decisive ruling. The plethora of conflicting opinion testifies to the realize of Amos's prophecy.

"...the Lord will dislodge before you [all these nations; you will dispossess nations greater and more numerous than you. Every spot on which your foot treads shall be yours;

your territory shall extend from the wilderness to the Lebanon, and from the River, the Euphrates, to the Western Sea. No man shall stand up to you: the Lord your God will put the dread and the fear of you over the whole land in which you set foot, as he promised you]" (Dt. 11:22-25):

Sifré to Deuteronomy L:III
1. A. Another matter concerning "...than you":
   B. Why is this stated? Has Scripture not in any case said, "Seven nations greater and mightier than you" (Dt. 7:1)?
   C. Why then does Scripture say, "...than you"?
   D. It indicates that any one of the seven peoples was greater and more intimidating than the whole of Israel.
   E. And so Scripture states, "Yet I destroyed the Amorites before them, whose height was like the height of the cedars, and who was strong as the oaks" (Amos 2:9).

Amos provides proof that the Israelites overcame, with God's help, mighty nations.

Sifré to Deuteronomy XCVI:V
1. A. "You shall not gash yourselves" (Dt. 14:1):
   B. [Since the letters for "gash yourselves" yield "form parties," we read:] You should not form parties, but all of you should form a single party.
   C. And so Scripture says, "He is the one who builds his upper chambers in heaven and has founded his party upon the earth" (Amos 9:6).

God favors a unified community and does not encourage partisanship. There is only one party founded by God on earth.

Sifré to Deuteronomy CCCXVII:I
1. A. ["He set him atop the highlands, to feast on the yield of the earth; he fed him honey from the crag, and oil from the flinty rock, curd of kine and milk of flocks; with the best of lambs and rams and he-goats, with the very finest wheat — and foaming grape-blood was your drink" (Dt. 32:13-14).]
   B. "...curd of kine and milk of flocks":
   C. This was in the time of Solomon:
   D. "Ten fat oxen, twenty oxen out of the pastures, and a hundred sheep" (1 Kgs. 5:3).
2. A. "...with the best of lambs and rams and he-goats":
   B. This was in the time of the ten tribes:
   C. "And eat the lambs out of the flock, and the calves out of the midst of the stall" (Amos 6:4).
3. A. "...with the very finest wheat — and foaming grape-blood was your drink":
   B. This was in the time of Solomon:

      C. "And Solomon's provision for one day was thirty measures of fine flour" (1 Kgs. 5:2).
4. A. "...and foaming grape-blood was your drink":
      B. This was in the time of the ten tribes:
      C. "That drink wine in bowls" (Amos 6:6).

The promises of Deuteronomy were kept in the time of the Ten Tribes, so Amos.

Sifré to Deuteronomy CCCXVIII:I

9. A. So you find in the case of the ten tribes, that they went into exile only out of an abundance of eating, drinking, and prosperity.
      B. For it is said, "That lie on beds of ivory, that drink wine in bowls...therefore now shall they go captive at the head of them who go captive" (Amos 6:4, 6, 7).

Amos prophesied that the Ten Tribes went into exile because they enjoyed too great prosperity. That is what encouraged them to sin, an implicit proposition here.

Sifré to Deuteronomy CCCXX:I

["The Lord saw and was vexed, and spurned his sons and his daughters. He said, 'I will hide my countenance from them and see how they fare in the end. For they are a treacherous breed, children with no loyalty in them. They incensed me with no-gods, vexed me with their futilities; I'll incense them with a no-people, vex them with a nation of fools. For a fire has flared in my wrath, and burned to the bottom of Sheol, has consumed the earth and its increase, eaten down to the base of the hills. I will sweep misfortunes on them, use up my arrows on them; wasting famine, ravaging plague, deadly pestilence, and fanged beasts will I let loose against them, with venomous creepers in dust. The sword shall deal wealth without, as shall the terror within, to youth and maiden alike, the suckling as well as the aged. I might have reduced them to naught, made their memory cease among men, but for fear of the taunts of the foe, their enemies who might misjudge and say, 'Our own hand has prevailed; none of this was wrought by the Lord!' For they are a folk void of sense, lacking in all discernment. Were they wise, they would think upon this, gain insight into their future. How could one have routed a thousand or two put ten thousand to flight, unless their rock had sold them, the Lord had given them up? For their rock is not like our rock, in our enemies' own estimation" (Dt. 32:19-31).]

5. A. "...children with no loyalty in them":
      B. "You are children without faith. You stood before Mount Sinai and said, 'Whatever the Lord has spoken we shall do and we shall hear' (Ex. 24:7). 'Then I said, 'you are god[like]' (Ps. 82:6).

C. "'When you said to the heifer, 'These are your gods O Israel' (Ex. 32:4), for my part I say, 'Therefore like man will you do' (Ps. 82:7).

D. "I brought you into the land of your ancestors and you built the chosen house for yourself, and I said that you will never go into exile from it.

E. "But when you said, 'We have no share in David' (2 Sam. 20:1), I for my part said, 'Israel will certainly go into exile from its land' (Amos 7:17).''

When the Israelites refused their share in David, God decided to send them into exile.

"[I thought I would make an end of them I might have made their memory cease among men, but for fear of the taunts of the foe, their enemies who might misjudge and say, 'Our own hand has prevailed; none of this was wrought by the Lord!' For they are a folk void of sense, lacking in all discernment. Were they wise, they would think upon this, gain insight into their future. How could one have routed a thousand or two put ten thousand to flight, unless their rock had sold them, the Lord had given them up? For their rock is not like our rock, in our enemies' own estimation" (Dt. 32:19-31).]

Sifré to Deuteronomy CCCXXII:III

1. A. "...their enemies who might misjudge":
   B. In the time of Israel's trouble, the nations of the world treat them as strangers and act as though they do not know them at all.
   C. And so we find that the wanted to flee toward the north, but they would not gather them in, rather closing the gates against them, in line with this verse:
   D. "For three sins of Tyre, and even for four, I shall not grant them a reprieve, because, forgetting the ties of kinship, they delivered a whole band of exiles to Edom" (Amos 1:9).
   E. They wanted to flee to the south but they shut them out:
   F. "Thus says the Lord, For three sins of Gaza, even for four, I shall grant them no reprieve, because they deported a whole band of exiles and delivered them up to Edom" (Amos 1:6).
   G. They wanted to flee to the east, but they shut them out:
   H. "Thus says the Lord, For three sins of Damascus...." (Amos 1:3).
   I. They wanted to flee to the west, but they shut them out:
   J. "With the Arabs: an oracle. You caravans of Dedan, that camp in the scrub with the Arabs, bring water to meet the thirsty. You dwellers in Tema, meet the fugitives with food, for they flee from the sword, the sharp edge of the sword, from the bent bow, and from the press of battle" (Is. 21;13-15).
   K. When things go well with Israel, the nations of the world try to deceive them and pretend that they are brothers, and so Esau said to Jacob, "I have more than enough, keep what is yours, my brother" (Gen. 33:).

L. And so did Hiram say to Solomon, "What are these forests, which you have given to me, my brother" (1 Kgs. 9:13).

The nations prevented the Israelites from taking refuge in their lands, thus Tyre, Gaza, and Damascus acted. The nations treat the Israelites as strangers when the Israelites are in trouble, so Amos.

Sifré to Deuteronomy CCCXXII:IV

1. A. "...and say, 'Our own hand has prevailed; none of this was wrought by the Lord!'":
   B. Just as those idiots said, "Have we not won power by our own strength" (Amos 6:13).

The Israelites do not acknowledge God's help, so Amos.

Sifré to Deuteronomy CCCXLII:I

1. A. "This is the blessing with which Moses, the man of God, bade the Israelites farewell before he died" (Dt. 33:1):
   B. Since Moses had earlier said to the Israelites harsh words, for example,
   C. "The wasting of hunger...without shall the sword bereave" (Dt. 32:24-5),
   D. "Also in Horeb you made the Lord angry" (Dt. 9:8),
   E. "You have been rebellious against the Lord" (Dt. 9:7),
   F. now he went and said to them words of comfort: "This is the blessing with which Moses, the man of God, bade the Israelites farewell before he died."
2. A. And from him did all of the prophets learn [how to conduct themselves].
   B. For they would first say to Israel harsh words and then go and say to them words of comfort.
   C. Now, for instance, you have among the prophets none whose words were more harsh than Hosea.
   D. When he began to speak, he said, "Give them, O Lord, whatever you will give. Give them a miscarrying womb" (Hos. 9:14)
   E. But then he spoke to them words of comfort:
   F. "His branches shall spread, his beauty shall be as the olive tree, and his fragrance as Lebanon. They who dwell under his shadow shall again make grain grown and shall blossom as the vine" (Hos. 144:7-8).
   G. "I will heal their backsliding, I will love them freely...I will be as the dew to Israel, he shall blossom as the lily" (Hos. 14:5-6).
3. A. So too Joel, to begin with: "Hear this, you old men, and give ear, all you inhabitants of the land. Has this been in your days or in the days of your fathers? Tell your children about it...that which the palmer-worm has left the locust has eaten" (Joel 1:2-4).

> B. At the end, he said these words of comfort: "And I will return to you the years that the locust has eaten, the canker worm and the caterpillar and the palmer-worm" (Joel 2:25).
> 4. A. So too Amos, to begin with: "Hear this word, you cows of Bashan, who are in the mountain of Samaria, who oppress the poor, crush the needy, say to their husbands, 'Bring that we may feast'" (Amos 4:1).
> B. At the end, he said these words of comfort: "Behold the days come...when the plowman will overtake the reaper" (Amos 9:13).
> 5. A. So too Micah, to begin with: "Who hate the good and love evil, who rob...who also eat the meat of my people and flay their skin off from them" (Mic. 3:2-3).
> B. At the end, he said these words of comfort: "Who is a God like you, who pardons the iniquity and ignores the transgression of the remnant of his heritage? He does not remain angry forever, because he delights in mercy. He will again have compassion upon us, he will subdue our iniquities and you will cast their sins into the depths of the sea. You will show faithfulness to Jacob, mercy to Abraham, as you have sworn to our fathers from the days of old" (Mic. 7:18-20).
> 6. A. So too Jeremiah, to begin with: "Then I will take away from the cities of Judah and the streets of Jerusalem the voice of mirth and the voice of gladness" (Jer. 7:34).
> B. At the end, he said these words of comfort: "Then will the virgin rejoice in the dance" (Jer. 31:13).
> 7. A. Might one think that once the prophets have said words of consolation, they then go and once again say words of rebuke?
> B. Scripture states, "And you shall say, 'Thus shall Babylon sink and not rise again, because of the evil that I will bring upon her...thus far as the words of Jeremiah'" (Jer. 51:64).
> C. That shows that once the prophets have said words of consolation, they do not then go and once again say words of rebuke.

Like other prophets, Amos began his prophesy with admonition but ended with consolation.

Sifré to Deuteronomy CCCLVII:XI

> 1. A. "[So Moses,] the servant of the Lord, [died there, in the land of Moab, at the command of the Lord. He buried him in the valley in the land of Moab, near Beth-peor, and no one knows his burial place to his day":
> B. [In calling Moses "the servant," it is not in derision of Moses that Scripture speaks, but rather in his praise.
> C. For so we find that the former prophets are called servants,
> D. as it is said, "For the Lord God will do nothing without revealing his plan to his servants the prophets" (Amos 3:7).

God calls the prophets servants.

Mekhilta Attributed to R. Ishmael

"The Lord said to Moses and Aaron in the land of Egypt, saying" (Ex. 12:1):

Mekhilta Attributed to R. Ishmael I:II.
- 1. A. Rabbi says, "'to Moses and Aaron' —
- 5. A. You may conclude that the Presence of God does not make an appearance outside of the land,
  - B. for it is said, "But Jonah rose up to flee to Tarshish from the presence of the Lord" (Jonah 1:3).
  - C. Now was he in fact fleeing from before the Lord? But is it not stated, "Where shall I go from your spirit?...If I ascend to heaven, you are there, if I make my bed in the nether world, lo, you are there, if I take the wings of the morning....even there would your hand lead me" (Ps. 139:7); "The eyes of the Lord, that run to and fro through the whole earth" (Zech. 4:10); "The eyes of the Lord are in every place, keeping watch upon the evil and the good" (Prov. 154:3); "Though they did into the netherworld...though they climb up to heaven...though they hide in the top of Carmel...though they go into captivity" (Amos. 9:2ff); "There is no darkness, nor shadow of death, where the workers of iniquity may hide themselves" (Job. 34:22).

God does not appear to Israel outside of the land, and Amos contributes to proof of that proposition.

- XI:I.1 A. ""Then Moses called all the elders of Israel:"
- 17. A. Another teaching concerning "For the Lord will pass [through to slay the Egyptians]:"
  - B. [Since the letters for "pass" can be read to mean "anger,"] the Lord will visit his anger and reason to fear him in Egypt,
  - C. and "anger" can mean only "wrath," as it is said, "He sent forth on them the fierceness of his anger, wrath, indignation, and trouble" (Ps. 78:49); "That day is a day of wrath" (Zeph. 1:15); "Behold the way of the Lord comes, cruel and full of wrath and fierce anger" (Is. 13:9); "And in all the vineyard shall be lamentation, for I will pass through in the midst of you, says the Lord" (Amos 5:17).

When God passes through the Land of Egypt, it is with anger, wrath, and indication.

Mekhilta Attributed to R. Ishmael XXI:I.
- 10. A. "stand firm, and see the salvation of the Lord:"
  - B. The Israelites said to him, "When?"
  - C. Moses said to them, "Today the Holy Spirit rests on you."

D. For the sense of the word "stand firm" in all passages is to encompass the Holy Spirit: "I saw the Lord standing beside the altar" (Amos 9:1). "The Lord came and stood and called as at other times, 'Samuel, Samuel'" (1 Sam. 3:10). "Call Joshua and stand in the tent of meeting that I may give him a charge" (Dt. 31:14).

Amos provides an example of the meaning of 'stand,' and that is to encompass the Holy Spirit in the transaction.

Mekhilta Attributed to R. Ishmael XXXI:II.
1. A. "you send forth your fury:"
4. A. This teaches you that there was no more despicable kingdom than the Egyptians, but it held power for a while, on account of the honor that is owing to Israel.
   B. When Scripture creates metaphors for the kingdoms, it compares them only to cedars: "Behold, the Assyrian was a cedar in Lebanon" (Ez. 31:3); "Yet I destroyed the Amorite before them, whose height was like the height of the cedars" (Amos 2:9); "The tree that you saw" (Dan. 4:17).
   C. But when Scripture creates metaphors for the Egyptians, it compares them only to stubble: "it consumes them like stubble."
   D. When Scripture creates metaphors for the kingdoms, it compares them only to silver and gold: "As for that image, its head was of fine gold" (Dan. 2:32).
   E. But when Scripture creates metaphors for the Egyptians, it compares them only to lead: "They sank like lead" (Ex. 15:10).
   F. When Scripture creates metaphors for the kingdoms, it compares them only to wild beasts: "And four great beasts" (Dan. 7:3).
   G. But when Scripture creates metaphors for the Egyptians, it compares them only to foxes: "Take us the foxes" (Song 2:15).
5. A. Antoninus asked our holy master, "I want to go to Alexandria. Can the city set up a king against me and defeat me?"
   B. He said to him, "I don't know. But it is written for us that the land of Egypt cannot set up either a ruler or a prince: 'And there shall be no more a prince out of the land of Egypt' (Ez. 30:13).
   C. "'It shall be the lowliest of the kingdoms' (Ez. 29:15)."

Amos provides an example of how God pays honor to the kingdoms, except to Egypt.

Mekhilta Attributed to R. Ishmael XXXV:I.
1 A. "You will bring them in and plant them [on your own mountain, the place O Lord, which you have made for your abode, the sanctuary, O Lord, which your hands have established. The Lord will reign forever and ever. For when the horses of Pharaoh with

2. Amos in Sifra...

his chariots and his horsemen went into the sea, the Lord brought back the waters of the sea upon them; but the people of Israel walked on dry ground in the midst of the sea]:"

3. A. Another interpretation of the clause, "You will bring them in and plant them:"
   B. ["...and plant them" in such a way that] there will be no plucking up:
   C. "And I will build them and not pull them down; and I will plant them and not pluck them up" (Jer. 24:6); "And I will plant them upon their land, and they shall no more be plucked up" (Amos 9:15).

Amos prophesies that when God plants Israel upon its Land, they will not again go into exile.

Mekhilta Attributed to R. Ishmael XXXV:II.

1. A. "Then Miriam, the prophetess, the sister of Aaron, took [a timbrel in her hand; and all the women went out after her with timbrels and dancing. And Miriam said to them, 'Sing to the Lord, for he has triumphed gloriously; the horse and his rider he has thrown into the sea]:"
   B. Where do we find that Miriam prophesied?
   C. She said to her father, "You are going to produce a son who will arise and save Israel from the power of Egypt."
   D. Forthwith: "There went a man of the house of Levi and took a wife...and the woman conceived and bore a son...and when she could not hide him any longer" (Ex. 2:1-3_.
   E. Her father berated her: "What has become of your prophecy?"
   F. But she held fast to her prophecy: "And his sister stood afar off, to know what would be done to him" (Ex. 2:4).
2. A. ["And his sister stood afar off, to know what would be done to him" (Ex. 2:4):] The sense of "standing" is only the Holy Spirit.
   B. For so it is said, "I saw the Lord standing beside the altar" (Amos 9:4); "And the Lord came and stood" (1 Sam. 3:10); "Call Joshua and stand" (Dt. 31:14).
3. A. "[And his sister stood] afar off, [to know what would be done to him]" (Ex. 2:4):
   B. The sense of "afar" is only the Holy Spirit:
   C. "From afar the Lord appeared to me" (Jer. 31:2).
4. A. "[And his sister stood afar off,] to know [what would be done to him]" (Ex. 2:4):
   B. The sense of "know" is only the Holy Spirit:
   C. "For the earth shall be full of the knowledge of the Lord" (Is. 11:9); For the earth shall be filled with the knowledge of the glory of the Lord, as the waters cover the sea" (Hab.. 2:14).
5. A. "[And his sister stood afar off, to know] what would be done to him" (Ex. 2:4):

B. The sense of "what would be done to him" is only the Holy Spirit:
C. "For the Lord will do nothing without revealing his counsel to his servants the prophets" (Amos 3:7).

The Holy Spirit is the source of God's revelation to the prophets of what he plans to do, so Amos.

Mekhilta Attributed to R. Ishmael L:I.
1. A. "And Mount Sinai was entirely wrapped in smoke:"
   B. Might one suppose that it was only the place of the glory [of God]?
   C. Scripture says, "entirely."
2. A. "because the Lord descended upon it in fire:"
   B. This indicates that the Torah is fire, given from fire, compared to fire.
   C. What happens with fire? If someone comes near it, one is burned; if someone goes to far from it, one freezes.
   D. One can only warm oneself by its flame.
3. A. "and the smoke of it went up like the smoke of a kiln:"
   B. Might one suppose it was like any sort of smoke?
   C. Scripture says, "of a kiln."
   D. Since it was like smoke of a kiln, might one suppose it was like that of a kiln only?
   E. Scripture says, "and the mountain burned with fire to the heart of heaven" (Dt. 4:11).
   F. If so, why does Scripture say, "of a kiln"?
   G. It is so as to open the ear by saying what the ear can hear.
4. A. Along these same lines: "The lion has roared, who will not fear" (Amos 3:8).
   B. Now who was it who gave strength and might to the lion? Is it not He?
   C. But thus he is described through the things that he has made, so as to open the ear by saying what the ear can hear.

God is described in terms that man can grasp, so is compared by Amos to the lion.

Mekhilta Attributed to R. Ishmael LII:I.
1. A. "You shall have no other gods before me" (Ex. 20:3):
9. A. When were they called by his name?
   B. In the time of Enosh, son of Seth. For it is said, "Then men began to call idols by the name of the Lord" (Gen. 4:26).
   C. Then the ocean went and covered a third of the world.
   D. Said to them the Holy One, blessed be He, "You have done a new thing on your own initiative in calling [idols by my name]. So I too shall do a new thing and on my own initiative I shall call [the ocean]."

E. So it is said, "Who calls for the waters of the sea and pours them out upon the face of the earth, the Lord is his name" (Amos 5:8).

See Sifré to Deuteronomy XLIII:VI

Mekhilta Attributed to R. Ishmael LXXIII:II.
1. A. "But if it is stolen from him, [he shall make restitution to its owner. If it is torn by beasts, let him bring it as evidence; he shall not make restitution for what has been torn]:"
6. A. "If it is torn by beasts, let him bring it as evidence; [he shall not make restitution for what has been torn]:"
   B. "That is, the hide," the words of R. Josiah.
   C. "Even though there is no direct proof, there is at least an indication: 'Thus says the Lord, as the shepherd rescues out of the mouth of the lion two legs or a piece of an ear' (Amos 3:12).
   D. R. Ahai b. R. Josiah says, "'If it is torn by beasts, let him bring it as evidence:' let him bring witnesses that it was torn and then he will be exempt from having to pay restitution."
   E. R. Jonathan says, "'If it is torn by beasts, let him bring it as evidence:' let him bring the owner to the torn beast and then he will be exempt from having to make restitution."

Amos indicates that the shepherd may bring evidence of loss of the beast to a wild animal and so exempt himself from paying for the loss.

3

Amos in the Yerushalmi

Yerushalmi Berakhot 2:3 [II:9]

[D] R. Idi b. R. Simeon in the name of R. Yohanan, "A person should not stand on a high place and pray." What is the Scriptural basis for this? Said R. Abba b. R. Papi, "Out of the depths I cry to thee, O Lord [Ps. 130:1]."

[E] Said R. Idi b. R. Simeon in the name of R. Yohanan, "A person should not stand up to pray if he needs to relieve himself." What is the Scriptural basis for this? "Prepare to meet your God, O Israel (Amos 4:12)."

[F] Said R. Alexander, "'Guard your feet when you go to the house of God' (Qoh. 4:17) — [means] guard yourself from the drops which fall from between your legs [when you urinate]."

Amos is taken to mean one should prepare to encounter God by voiding.

Yerushalmi Shabbat 6:9 [III:1

A] R. Samuel, R. Abbahu in the name of R. Yohanan: "Whatever serves to bring healing is not prohibited on the count of 'the ways of the Amorite' [M. 6:10D-E]"

[B] He who says, *"Dargan, Qardan,"* lo, this is one of "the ways of the Amorites."

[C] R. Judah says, "They may say *Dagan* on account of the idol of that name,

[D] "since it says, '[Now the lords of the Philistines, gathered to offer a great sacrifice] to Dagan their god, and to rejoice' (Judg. 16:23)."

[E] He who says, *"Dani, Dano,"* lo, this is one of "the ways of the Amorites."

[F] R. Judah says, "This is because of the idol, *Dan,*

[G] "since it says, 'As thy god lives, O Dan,' and 'As the way of Beersheba lives' (Amos 8:14)" [T. Shab. 7:2-3].

The Toseftan passage is reproduced.

Yerushalmi Taanit 3:3

[A] And so too: A town on which rain did not fall,

[B] as it is said, "And I caused it to rain upon one city and caused it not to rain upon another city, one piece was rained upon and the piece on which it rained not did wither" (Amos 4:7)

[C] that town declares a fast day and sounds the shofar. .

[D] And all its neighbors fast but do not sound the shofar.

[E] R. Aqiba says, "They sound the shofar but do not fast."

[I:1 A] Said R. Simeon, "It is written, 'And I caused it to rain upon one city, and caused it not to rain upon another city, one piece was rained upon, and the piece on which it rained not did wither' (Amos 4:7): *the merit associated with a particular field is what did it.*"

Amos's formulation is given a close reading.

Yerushalmi Taanit 1:9 II:5

A   R. Ada b. R. Simeon in the name of R. Yohanan: "A man should not stand to pray in an elevated place."

[B] What is the scriptural basis for this view?

[C] Said R. Ba in the name of R. Pappa, "'Out of the depths I cry to thee, O Lord!'" (Ps. 130:1).

[D] R. Ada bar Simeon in the name of R. Yohanan: "A man should not stand to pray prior to heeding a call to nature."

[E] What is the scriptural basis for this view?

[F] "[Therefore thus I will do to you, O Israel; because I will do this to you,] prepare to meet your God, O Israel!" (Amos 4:12).

[G] Said R. Simon, "[Reading the word, 'prepare,' as 'pay heed to':] Form the appropriate intention to 'meet your God, O Israel.'"

[H] Said R. Alexandri, "'Guard your feet when you go to the house of God' (Qoh. 5:1). Guard yourself with regard to the things that come forth between your feet."

[I] That which you have said applies to the lesser matters [one must urinate], but as to the more sizable matters, if one can endure, let him endure [until after the prayer].

The Tosefta's passage is echoed.

Yerushalmi Hagigah 2:1 [II:1

A] Nor the Work of Creation to two

[D] *R. Judah bar Pazzi sat teaching,* "In the beginning the world consisted of water upon water."

[E] R. Judah bar Pazzi expounded, "In the beginning the world consisted of water [heaped] on water." *That indicates that the law accords with the view of R. Ishmael.*

3. Amos in the Yerushalmi

[F] *What is the proof?* "And the Spirit/Wind of God moved over the face of the waters" (Gen. 1:2).

[G] Then he made the snow — "He casts forth his ice like morsels" (Ps. 147:17).

[H] Then he made the earth — "For to the snow he says, 'Become earth'" (Job 37:6).

[I] And the earth stands on the waters: "To him who spread out the earth on the waters" (Ps. 136:6).

[J] And the waters stand on the mountains: "The waters stood over the mountains" (Ps. 104: 6).

[K] And the mountains stand on the wind: "For behold, he forms the mountains and creates the wind" (Amos 4:13).

[L] And the air depends on the storm-wind: "The storm-wind fulfills his command" (Ps. 148:8).

[M] The Holy One, blessed be he, made the storm-wind like a sort of amulet suspended from his arm, as it is said, "And underneath are the arms of the world" (Deut. 33:27).

[N] "For behold, he forms the mountains" — this is one of the six biblical passages over which Rabbi wept while reading them: "Seek the Lord, all you humble of the earth" (Zeph. 2:3), "Hate evil, and love good" (Amos 5:15), "Let him put his mouth in the dust" (Lam. 3:29), "For God will bring every evil deed into judgment" (Qoh. 12:14), "And Samuel said to Saul, 'Why have you provoked me?'" (1 Sam. 28:15).

[O] [As to the last of these, the relevance of which is shown in a moment,] Samuel said to him, "You have succeeded only in provoking your creator against me. You have made me your idol. Do you not know that just as they punish him who serves [an idol], so they punish him who is worshipped? But even more, I thought that it was the Day of Judgment, and I was afraid."

[P] Are not the words an argument *a minori ad maius:* just as Samuel, the chief of the prophets, about whom it is written, "And all Israel from Beersheba to Dan knew" (1 Sam. 3:20), was afraid of the Day of Judgment, how much more should we fear it!

[Q] The argument is supported by [the following verse: "He forms the hills and creates the wind" (Amos 4:13). Even matters that are not sinful are inscribed against a man upon his [heavenly] tablet.

[R] And who tells man? The breath from his mouth.

[S] R. Haggai in the name of R. Yabes: "'He forms the hills and creates the wind/breath'" (Amos 4:13)

[T] *R. Haggai also in the name of R. Yabes: "These men of Sepphoris [say that the word tohu] means 'darkness' and 'a gloomy place.'"*

[U] R. Judah bar Pazzi in the name of R. Yosé b. R. Judah: "*Hadrian asked the proselyte Aqila, 'Is it true that you [Jews] say that the world is suspended on air?' 'Yes,' said Aqila.*

[V] *"Hadrian said to him, 'How will you prove it to me?'*

[W] "Aqila said to him, 'Bring me young camels.' He brought him young camels. He loaded and raised them up. He made them sink down, took them and strangled them.

[X] "He said to Hadrian, 'See your camels, raise them up!'

[Y] "Hadrian said, 'After you have strangled them!'

[Z] "He said to him, 'What do they lack except the air that has gone out of them?'"

Amos contributes to an account of cosmology, K. Amos further is read to maintain that God pays attention to the most benign actions of people.

Yerushalmi Moed Qatan 3:3 [I:13

[A] Whence in the Torah do we derive the rites of mourning?

[B] As to the observance of seven days: "And he made a mourning for his father seven days" (Gen. 50:10).

[C] Do they derive a law from evidence pertaining to the period prior to the giving of the Torah?

[D] *R. Jacob bar Aha in the name of R. Zeira: "Derive the rule from the following:* 'At the door of the tent of meeting you shall remain day and night for seven days, performing what the Lord has charged, lest you die' (Lev. 8:35).

[E] "Just as the Holy One, blessed be he, kept watch over his world for seven days, so you must keep watch for your brothers for seven days."

[F] And how do we know that the Holy One, blessed be he, kept watch over his world for seven days?

[G] "And after seven days the waters of the flood came upon the earth" (Gen. 7:10).

[H] But do they mourn prior to the death of the deceased [before the flood]?

[I] But the answer is simple: In the case of mortal man, who does not know what is going to happen, one undertakes the rites of mourning only after the person has died.

[J] But in the case of the Holy One, blessed be he, who knows what is going to happen, he kept watch over his world from the very beginning [even before the world perished in the flood].

[K] *There is he who proposes to state:* This refers to the seven days of mourning for Methuselah, the righteous.

[L] Said R. Hoshaiah, "'[And do not go out from the door of the tent of meeting, lest you die;] for the anointing oil of the Lord is upon you. [And they did according to the word of Moses]' (Lev. 10:7). Just as you have been anointed with the anointing oil for seven days, so you must keep watch for your [deceased] brethren for seven days."

[M] R. Abbahu in the name of R. Yohanan: "'Let her not be as one dead[, of whom the flesh is half consumed when he comes out of his mother's womb. And Moses cried to the Lord, Heal her, O

3. Amos in the Yerushalmi

God, I beseech thee]' (Num. 12:12-13). Let her be shut up. Just as the days of mourning for the deceased are seven, so the days of shutting up [for the inspection of leprosy signs] are to be seven."

[N] *A disciple repeated this statement of R. Yohanan before R. Simeon b. Laqish, who did not accept it. He said, "Here you deal with a case of shutting up, while there you deal with a case of certifying that a person is unclean."*

[O] For R. Yohanan in the name of R. Yannai: "'Let her not be as one dead' (Num. 12:12). Just as the seven days of mourning for the deceased do not count [toward the days of observing the Nazirite vow], so the days of being certified unclean do not count [toward the thirty days of observance of the Nazirite vow] ."

[P] R. Jeremiah and R. Hiyya in the name of R. Simeon b. Laqish, R. Abbahu, R. Yosé b. Haninah in the name of R. Simeon b. Laqish: "'And the people of Israel wept for Moses in the plains of Moab thirty days; then the days of weeping and mourning for Moses were ended' (Deut. 34:8). 'The days' refers to the seven days of mourning. 'Weeping' is two. 'Mourning' is thirty."

[Q] *And there are those who revise the matter as follows:* "Days" is two, "weeping" is seven, and "mourning" is thirty.

[R] R. Yosé, R. Hiyya in the name of R. Simeon b. Laqish, R. Jonah and R. Hiyya and R. Simeon b. Laqish in the name of R. Yudan the Patriarch: "'I will turn your feasts into mourning [and all your songs into lamentation; I will bring sackcloth upon all loins and baldness on every head; I will make it like the mourning for an only son, and the end of it like a bitter day]' (Amos 8:10). Just as the days of the Festival [of Tabernacles] are seven, so the days of mourning are seven."

[S] Said R. Ammi to R. Hiyya bar Ba, "Perhaps we may say, 'Just as the days of the Festival [of Tabernacles] are eight, so the days of mourning are eight'?"

Amos contributes to the formation of the law the proof that the days of mourning are seven by analogy to the days of the Festival of Tabernacles, feasts into mourning beyond the key language.

Yerushalmi Sotah 1:9

[A] And so is it on the good side:

[B] Miriam waited a while for Moses, since it is said, And his sister stood afar off (Ex. 2:4), therefore, Israel waited on her seven days in the wilderness, since it is said, And the people did not travel on until Miriam was brought in again (Num. 12:15).

[I:1 A] Said R. Yohanan, "The following verse was stated through the Holy Spirit: 'And his sister stood at a distance, [to know what would be done to him]' (Ex. 2:4)."

[C] "I saw the Lord standing beside the altar" (Amos 9:1). .

[D] **His sister:** "Say to wisdom, You are my sister" (Prov. 7:4).

[E] **From a distance:** "The Lord appeared to him from afar" (Jer. 31:3).
[F] **To know:** "The earth shall be full of the knowledge of the Lord [as the waters cover the sea]'" (Is. 11:9).
[G] **What would be done to him:** "Surely the Lord does nothing, without revealing his secret to his servants the prophets'" (Amos 3:7).

Amos 3:7 clarifies the sense of Ex. 2:4, Miriam being a prophet, who would know what was to happen.

Yerushalmi Sotah 9:15 9:13

[A] When the former prophets died out, the Urim and Tummim were cancelled.
[B] **When the sanctuary was destroyed, the Shamir-worm ceased and [so did] the honey of supim.**
[II:1A] **When the sanctuary was destroyed, the Shamir-worm ceased:**
[B] Said R. Judah, "What is the character of this worm? It is a creature from the six days of Creation. When they put it on stones or on beams, they are opened up before it like the pages of a notebook. And not only so, but when they put it on iron, [the iron] is split and falls apart before it. And nothing can stand before it.
[C] **"How is it kept? They wrap it in tufts of wool and put it in a lead tube full of barley-bran."** [Yerushalmi adds: This is in line with the verse, 'The Lord is his name, who makes destruction flash forth against the strong, so that destruction comes upon the fortress' (Amos 5:9)." [T. Sot. 15:1].

Amos provides a proof-text.

Yerushalmi Abodah Zarah 1:1

[A] [39a] **Before the festivals of gentiles for three days it is forbidden to do business with them,**
[B] **[1] to lend anything to them or to borrow anything from them,**
[C] **[2] to lend money to them or to borrow money from them,**
[D] **[3] to repay them or to be repaid by them.**
[I:1 A] *R. Hama bar Uqbah derived scriptural support for all of those [statements about the interval of three days during which it is prohibited to do business with gentiles prior to a festival of theirs] from the following verse:* "[Come to Bethel and transgress; to Gilgal and multiply transgression;] bring your sacrifices every morning, your tithes on the third day" (Amos 4:4).
[B] *Said to him R. Yosé, "If so, then even in the exilic communities [the rule should be the same].*
[C] *"Yet it has been taught in a Tannaitic tradition:* **'Nahum the Mede says, "One day in the exilic communities [before their festival] it is prohibited [to do business with gentiles, and not the three**

3. Amos in the Yerushalmi

days specified by M. A.Z. 1:1, which apply only to the Holy Land]"' [T. A.Z. 1:1A]."

[D] *Why so?*
[E] *There* [in Babylonia] they looked into the matter and found out that [the pagans] prepare their requirements [for celebrating a festival] in only a single day, so they forbade business dealings with them for a single day. *But here* [in the Holy Land] they looked into the matter and found out that they prepare their requirements [for celebrating a festival] in a full three days, so they forbade business dealings with them for a full three days.
[F] *How then does R. Yosé interpret the cited verse of Scripture,* "Bring your sacrifices every morning [etc.]"?
[G] Concerning the reign of Jeroboam does Scripture speak.
[H] Once Jeroboam took up the reign over Israel, he began to entice Israel [toward idolatry], saying to them, "Come and let us practice idolatrous worship. Idolatry is permissive."
[I] *That is the meaning of the following verse of Scripture:* "[Because Syria with Ephraim and the son of Remaliah has devised evil against you, saying,] 'Let us go up against Judah and terrify it, and let us conquer it for ourselves and set up the son of Tabeel as king in the midst of it'" (Is. 7:5-6).
[J] Said R. Abba, "We have searched through the whole of Scripture and have found no instance in which his name was Tabeel. But [the meaning is] that he does good for those who serve him."
[K] The Torah has said, "I chose him [the tribe of Levi] out of all the tribes of Israel to be my priest, to go up to my altar, to burn incense, to wear an ephod before me (1 Sam. 2:28)."
[L] And idolatry says, "[He also made houses on high places,] and appointed priests from the fringe element [MQSWT] of the people[, who were not of the Levites] (1 Kings 12:31)."
[M] Said Rabbi, "Not from the thorns [QWSYM] that were among the people, but from the refuse [PSWLT] that was among the people."
[N] The Torah has said, "You shall not let the fat of my feast remain until the morning" (Ex. 23:18).
[O] But idolatry has said, "Bring your sacrifices every morning" (Amos 4:4).
[P] The Torah has said, "[When you offer a sacrifice of peace-offerings to the Lord, you shall offer it so that you may be accepted]. It shall be eaten the same day you offer it, or on the morrow[; and anything left over until the third day shall be burned with fire]" (Lev. 19:5-6). [Q] And idolatry has said, ". . . your tithes on the third day" (Amos 4:4).
[Q] The Torah has said, "You shall not offer the blood of my sacrifice with leavened bread" (Ex. 23:18).
[R] And idolatry has said, "Offer a sacrifice of thanksgiving of that which is leavened" (Amos 4:5).

[S] The Torah has said, "When you make a vow to the Lord, your God, you shall not be slack to pay for it[; for the Lord your God will surely require it of you, and it would be a sin in you. But if you refrain from vowing, it shall be no sin in you. You shall be careful to perform what has passed your lips, for you have voluntarily vowed to the Lord your God what you have promised with your mouth]" (Deut. 23:21-23).

[T]] And idolatry has said, "And proclaim freewill offerings, publish them" (Amos 4:5).

[U] Said R. Yudan, father of R. Matteniah, "The intention of [a verse of] Scripture [such as is cited below] was only to make mention of the evil traits of [39b] Israel. 'On the day of our king [when Jeroboam was made king] the princes became sick with the heat of wine; he stretched out his hand with mockers' (Hosea 7:5).

[V] "On the day on which Jeroboam began to reign over Israel, *all Israel came to him at dusk, saying to him,* 'Rise up and worship idolatry.'

[W] *"He said to them, 'It is already dusk. I am partly drunk and partly sober, and the whole people is drunk. But if you want, go and come back in the morning.'*

[X] *"This is the meaning of the following Scripture,* 'For like an oven their hearts burn with intrigue; all night their anger smolders[; in the morning it blazes like a flaming fire]' (Hosea 7:6)."

[Y] "'All night their anger smolders.'

[Z] "'In the morning it blazes like a flaming fire.'

[AA] *"In the morning they came to him. Thus did he say to them, 'I know full well what you want, but I'm afraid of your sanhedrin, lest it come and kill me.'*

[BB] *"They said to him, 'We shall kill them.'*

[CC] *"That is the meaning of the following verse:* 'All of them are hot as an oven. And they devour their rulers' (Hos. 7:7)."

[DD] *[Concurring with this view,] R. Levi said, "They slew them. Thus do you read in Scripture [to prove that 'the princes became sick' (HHL) means 'the princes killed' (HLL)],* 'If anyone is found slain [HLL] (Deut. 21:1).'"

[EE] Rabbi does not [concur. He maintains that] they removed them from their positions of power [but did not kill them].

[FF] "On the day of our king the princes became sick with the heat of wine" (Hosea 7:5) — it was the day on which the princes be came sick.

[GG] What made them sick? It was the heat of the wine, for they were thirsting for wine.

[HH] "He stretched out his hand with the mockers." —

[II] *When he would see an honorable man, he would set up against him two mockers, who would say to him,* "Now what generation do you think is the most cherished of all generations?"

[JJ] He would answer them, "It was the generation of the wilderness [which received the Torah]."

[KK] *They would say to him, "Now did they themselves not worship an idol?"*

[LL] *And he would answer them, "Now do you think that, because they were cherished, they were not punished for their deed?"*

[MM] *And they would say to him, "Shut up! The king wants to do exactly the same thing. Not only so, but [the generation of the wilderness] only made one [calf], while [the king] wants to make two."*

[NN] "[So the king took counsel and made two calves of gold] and he set up one in Bethel, and the other he put in Dan (1 Kings 12:29)."

[OO] The arrogance of Jeroboam is what condemned him decisively [or: certified him as a leper].

[PP] Said R. Yosé bar Jacob, "It was at the conclusion of a sabbatical year that Jeroboam began to rule over Israel. That is the meaning of the following verse: '[And Moses commanded them.] At the end of every seven years, at the set time of the year of release, at the feast of booths, when all Israel comes to appear before the Lord your God at the place which he will choose, you shall read this law before all Israel in their hearing' (Deut. 31:10-11).

[QQ] *"[Jeroboam] said, 'I shall be called upon to read [the Torah, as Scripture requires]. If I get up and read first, they will say to me, 'The king of the place [in which the gathering takes place, namely, Jerusalem] comes first.' And if I read second, it is disrespectful to me. And if I do not read at all, it is a humiliation for me. And, finally, if I let the people go up, they will abandon me and go over to the side of Rehoboam the son of Solomon.'*

[RR] *"That is the meaning of the following verse of Scripture:* '[And Jeroboam said in his heart, "Now the kingdom will turn back to the house of David;] if this people go up to offer sacrifices in the house of the Lord at Jerusalem, then the heart of this people will turn again to their Lord, to Rehoboam, king of Judah, and they will kill me and return to Rehoboam, king of Judah"' (1 Kings 12:27-28).

[SS] "What then did he do? 'He made two calves of gold' (1 Kings 12:28), and he inscribed on their heart, '... lest they kill you' [as counsel to his successors].

[TT] "He said, 'Let every king who succeeds me look upon them.'"

[UU] Said R. Huna, "'[The wicked go astray from the womb, they err from their birth speaking lies. They have venom like the venom of a serpent, like the deaf adder that stops its ear, so that it does not hear the voice of charmers] or of the cunning caster of spells' (Ps. 58:5). Over whoever was associated with him [Jeroboam] he [Jeroboam] cast a spell [in the sin of the bull-calves]."

[VV] Said R. Huna, "'[Hearken, O house of the king! For the judgment pertains to you; for you have been a snare at Mizpah, and a net spread upon Tabor.] And they have made deep the pit of Shittim[, but I will chastise all of them]' (Hos. 5:1-2). For [Jeroboam] deepened the sin. He said, 'Whoever explains [the meaning of what has been inscribed on the bull-calves] I shall kill.'"

[WW] Said R. Abin bar Kahana, "Also in regard to the Sabbaths and the festivals we find that Jeroboam invented them on his own. That is the meaning of the following verse: 'And Jeroboam appointed a feast on the fifteenth day of the eighth month like the feast that was in Judah, and he offered sacrifices upon the altar[; so he did in Bethel, sacrificing to the calves that he had made]' (1 Kings 12:32).

[XX] "Thus he did in Bethel, having sacrifices made in a month that he made up on his own. This is as you read in Scripture, 'In addition to the Sabbaths of the Lord' (Lev. 23:23). [So Jeroboam confused the people by establishing his own calendar for Bethel, keeping the people from pilgrimages to Jerusalem in such a way.]"

The reference to "the third day" at Amos 4:4 indicates the interval during which it is prohibited to deal with gentiles in connection with their festivals. That is because the gentiles take three full days to prepare for celebrating a festival. The contrast between gentile and Israelite offerings is drawn, in part, through the same verse of Amos.

Yerushalmi Niddah 3:2 [III:2

A] **Said R. Hanina son of R. Abbahu, "The reason of R. Meir is that Scripture refers to these other things with the word form just as in the case of man: 'Then the Lord God formed man of dust from the ground' (Gen. 2:7)."**

[B] R. Ammi asked, "Now the word form [indeed] is written concerning domesticated cattle: 'So out of the ground the Lord God formed every beast of the field and every bird of the air' (Gen. 2:19). But lo, it is written, 'For lo, he who forms the mountains and creates the wind [and declares to man what is his thought, who makes the morning darkness and treads on the heights of the earth — the Lord, the God of hosts, is his name]' (Amos 4:13). On the basis of this verse [by the reasoning just now spelled out], if a woman aborted something in the shape of a mountain, she should be unclean."

God forms mountains, and things analogous to mountains, e.g., an abortion.

4

Amos in Genesis Rabbah, Leviticus Rabbah, and Pesiqta deRab Kahana

Genesis Rabbah

Genesis Rabbah I:IX.

1. A. A philosopher asked Rabban Gamaliel, saying to him, "Your God was indeed a great artist, but he had good materials to help him."
   B. He said to him, "What are they?"
   C. He said to him, "Unformed [space], void, darkness, water, wind, and the deep."
   D. He said to him, "May the spirit of that man [you] burst! All of them are explicitly described as having been created by him [and not as pre-existent].
   E. "Unformed space and void: 'I make peace and create evil' (Is. 45:7).
   F. "Darkness: 'I form light and create darkness' (Is. 45:7).
   G. "Water: 'Praise him, you heavens of heavens, and you waters that are above the heavens' (Ps. 148:4). Why? 'For he commanded and they were created' (Ps. 148:5).
   H. "Wind: 'for lo, he who forms the mountains creates the wind' (Amos 4:13).
   I. "The depths: 'When there were no depths, I was brought forth' (Prov. 8:24)."

Amos proves that God created the wind, which did not come into existence before creation.

Genesis Rabbah V:VI.

1. A. Said R. Eleazar, "From the beginning of the creation of the world the Holy One, blessed be he, made a decree and said, 'Let the water be gathered together under the heaven' (Gen. 1:9).
   B. "Why [is it written], 'Who calls for the waters of the sea,' 'and pours them out on the face of the earth' [stated two times, once at Amos 5:8, the other time at Amos 9:6]?
   C. "One refers to the generation of Enosh and the other to the generation of the dispersion."

Amos repeats his reference to God's calling and pouring the water on the face of the earth to speak of the generations of Enosh and of the dispersion. This speaks of two floods.

Genesis Rabbah XXIII:VII.

4. A. R. Abbahu gave an exposition, "The ocean is higher than the entire world."
   B. Said to him R. Eleazar b. Menahem, "And is this not the statement of a verse of Scripture: 'He calls forth the waters of the sea and pours them out upon the face of the earth' (Amos 5:8, 9:6), that is to say, like one who pours from above to below."
   C. It is written, "Who calls for the waters of the sea" in two separate passages.
   D. These two references correspond to the two times that the sea came up and covered the face of the world.
   E. And up to what point did the water come on the first occasion, and up to what point on the second occasion?
   F. R. Yudan and R. Abbahu, R. Eleazar in the name of R. Hanina: "On the first occasion the water came up to Acre and Jaffa, and on the second occasion it came up to the coast of Barbary."
   G. R. Huna and R. Aha in the name of R. Hanina, "On the first occasion it came up to the coast of Barbary and on the second occasion up to Acre and Jaffa.
   H. "That is in line with the following verse: 'And he said, "Thus far shall you come, but no further"' (Job 38:11).
   I. "'Thus far shall you come,' namely, up to Acre, 'and here shall your proud waves be stayed' (Job 38:11), up to Jaffa [a play on the words at hand]."
   J. R. Eleazar: "On the first occasion the water came as far as Calabria, and on the second occasion as far as the coasts of Barbary."

As in the preceding, so here Amos refers to two floods of the oceans over the land.

Genesis Rabbah XXV:II.

1. A. "[When Lamech had lived a hundred and eighty-two years, he became the father of a son,] and called his name Noah, saying, ['Out of the ground which the Lord has cursed this one shall bring us relief from our work and from the toil of our hands']" (Gen. 5:29):
   B. R. Yohanan said, "The name has no bearing on the interpretation that is given to it, and the interpretation has no bearing on the name. [The explanation does not fit the name that is explained.]
   C. "Either the Scripture should have said, 'This one will give us rest' [using the root NH, corresponding to the name Noah], or the text should have said, 'He called his name Nahman,' for 'this one will give us relief.' [The explanation given in the Scripture is for the name Nahman, not the name Noah.] But is it possible that the name Noah corresponds to the explanation, 'give us relief'? [Surely not.]
   D. "But when the Holy One, blessed be he, created man, he gave him rule over all things. The ploughing heifer obeyed the ploughman, the furrow obeyed the plough. But when man sinned, all things rebelled against him. The ploughing heifer would not obey the ploughman, and the furrow would not obey the plough. When Noah arose, they eased [their rebellion]. [How do we know it?]
   E. "The word for 'ease' occurs here [in the name Noah], and the word for 'ease' occurs in the following: 'So that your ox and your ass may have ease' (Ex. 23:12). Just as the 'ease' that is stated later on refers to 'ease' for an ox, so the word for 'ease' that is used here also refers to the ease of the ox."
   F. R. Simeon b. Laqish said, "The name has no bearing on the interpretation, and the interpretation has no bearing on the name.
   G. "Either the Scripture should have said, 'This one will give us rest' [using the root NH, corresponding to the name Noah], or the text should have said, 'He called his name Nahman,' for 'this one will give us relief.' [The explanation given in the Scripture is for the name Nahman, not the name Noah.]
   H. "But before Noah arose, the water would come up and flood the dead in their graves, for it is written two times in Scripture: 'He calls forth the waters of the sea and pours them out upon the face of the earth' (Amos 5:8, 9:6), corresponding to the two times a day on which the water would come up and flood out the dead in their graves, once in the morning, once in the evening, in line with this verse: 'Like the slain that lie in the grave' (Ps. 88:6). Even those who were lying in the grave were as if they had been slain. But when Noah arose, they enjoyed rest.
   I. "Here the word 'ease' written, and elsewhere it is written, 'For he enters into peace, they rest in their beds' (Is. 57:2). Just as in that passage, the reference is to the rest of the grave, so here too the meaning is the rest of the grave."

Yet another explanation of the repeated reference to God's calling up the waters is offered, now a flood morning and night. Noah finally allowed them to settle down.

Genesis Rabbah XXV:III.

1. A. "[And called his name Noah, saying,] 'Out of the ground which the Lord has cursed[this one shall bring us relief from our work and from the toil of our hands]'" (Gen. 5:29): [The curse was a famine, as will now be spelled out.]
   B. Ten famines came into the world.
   C. One was in the time of Adam: "Cursed is the ground for your sake" (Gen. 3:17).
   D. One was in the time of Lamech: "Out of the ground which the Lord has cursed" (Gen. 5:29).
   E. One was in the time of Abraham: "And there was a famine in the land" (Gen. 12:10).
   F. One was in the time of Isaac: "And there was famine in the land, beside the first famine that was in the time of Abraham (Gen. 26:1).
   G. One was in the time of Jacob: "For these two years has the famine been in the land" (Gen. 45:6).
   H. One was in the time of the rule of judges: "And it came to pass in the days when the judges ruled, that there was a famine in the land" (Ruth 1:1).
   I. One was in the time of David: "There was a famine in David's time" (2 Sam. 21:1).
   J. One was in the time of Elijah: "As the Lord, the God of Israel, lives, before whom I stand, there shall not be dew or rain these years" (1 Kgs. 17:1).
   K. One was in the time of Elisha: "And there was a great famine in Samaria" (2 Kgs. 6:25).
   L. There is one famine which moves about the world.
   M. One famine will be in the age to come: "Not a famine of bread nor a thirst for water but of hearing the words of the Lord" (Amos 8:11).

Amos speaks of a famine in the age to come.

Genesis Rabbah XXXI:III.

1. A. "They hate the one who reproves in the gate and abhor the one who speaks uprightly" (Amos 5:10).
   B. For he would say to them, "Fools, you abandon the one whose voice breaks the cedars and bow down to petrified wood."
   C. And because they were overstuffed with thievery, they were destroyed from the world, as it is said, "And God said to Noah, 'The end of all flesh is come before me, for the earth is filled with violence through them'" Gen. 6:13):

Amos condemns those that abandon God, whose voice breaks cedars, and bow down to pieces of wood.

Genesis Rabbah XL:III.
1. A. "Now there was a famine in the land" (Gen. 12:10):
   B. Ten famines came into the world.
   C. One was in the time of the first man [Adam]: "Cursed is the ground for your sake" (Gen. 3:17).
   D. One was in the time of Lamech: "Out of the ground which the Lord has cursed" (Gen. 5:29).
   E. One was in the time of Abraham: "And there was a famine in the land" (Gen. 12:10)
   F. One was in the time of Isaac: "And there was famine in the land, beside the first famine that was in the time of Abraham" (Gen. 26:1).
   G. One was in the time of Jacob: "For these two years has the famine been in the land" (Gen. 45:6).
   H. One was in the time of the rule of judges: "And it came to pass in the days when the judges ruled, that there was a famine in the land" (Ruth 1:1).
   I. One was in the time of David: "And there was a famine in the days of David" (2 Sam. 21:1).
   J. One was in the time of Elijah: "As the Lord, the God of Israel, lives, before whom I stand, there shall not be dew or rain these years" (1 Kgs. 17:1).
   K. One was in the time of Elisha: "And there was a great famine in Samaria" (2 Kgs. 6:25).
   L. There is one famine which moves about the world.
   M. One famine will be in the age to come: "Not a famine of bread nor a thirst for water but of hearing the words of the Lord" (Amos 8:11).

As above.

Genesis Rabbah XLIX:II.
1. A. [Referring to God's telling Abraham what he is about to do:] "The secret of the Lord is with them who fear him and his covenant to make them know it" (Ps. 25:14).
   B. To begin with "The secret of the Lord is with them who fear him" but in the end it was with the upright: "But his secret is with the upright" (Ps. 3:32).
   C. Then it is with the prophets: "For the Lord God will do nothing without revealing his secret to his servants the prophets" (Amos 3:7).
   D. Said the Holy One, blessed be he, "This Abraham fears God: 'Now I know that you are a God-fearing man' (Gen. 22:12).

E. "This Abraham is upright: 'The upright love you' (Song 1:4).
F. "This Abraham is a prophet: 'Now therefore restore the man's wife, for he is a prophet' (Gen. 20:7).
G. "Shall I not reveal it to him?"
H. "The Lord said, 'Shall I hide from Abraham [what I am about to do, seeing that Abraham shall become a great and mighty nation and all the nations of the earth shall bless themselves by him? No, for I have chosen him that he may charge his children and his household after him to keep the way of the Lord by doing righteousness and justice...']" (Gen. 17:17-19).

God reveals his secrets to the prophets.

Genesis Rabbah LXIV:II.

3. A. "Now there was a famine in the land" Gen. 16:1):
   B. Ten famines came into the world.
   C. One was in the time of Adam: "Cursed is the ground for your sake" (Gen. 3:17).
   D. One was in the time of Lamech: "Out of the ground which the Lord has cursed" (Gen. 5:29).
   E. One was in the time of Abraham: "And there was a famine in the land" (Gen. 12:10).
   F. One was in the time of Isaac: "And there was famine in the land, beside the first famine that was in the time of Abraham" (Gen. 26:1).
   G. One was in the time of Jacob: "For these two years has the famine been in the land" (Gen. 45:6).
   H. One was in the time of the rule of judges: "And it came to pass in the days when the judges ruled, that there was a famine in the land" (Ruth 1:1).
   I. One was in the time of Elijah: "As the Lord, the God of Israel, lives, before whom I stand, there shall not be dew or rain these years" (1 Kgs. 17:1).
   J. One was in the time of Elisha: "And there was a great famine in Samaria" (2 Kgs. 6:25).
   K. There is one famine which moves about the world.
   L. One famine will be in the age to come: "Not a famine of bread nor a thirst for water but of hearing the words of the Lord" (Amos 8:11).

As above.

Genesis Rabbah LXVII:X.

1. A. "Now therefore my son, obey my voice; arise, flee to Laban my brother in Haran, and stay with him a few days, [until your brother's fury turns away; until your brother's anger turns away, and he forgets what you have done to him; then I will send and fetch you

4. Amos in Genesis Rabbah, Leviticus Rabbah, and Pesiqta deRab Kahana

from there. Why should I be bereft of you both in one day?']" (Gen. 27:42-45):

2. A. "...until your brother's fury turns away:"
   B. His mother, righteous woman that she was, said, "Until your brother's fury turns away" [because she could not imagine that he would bear a grudge forever].
   C. But Esau, for his part, was not that way: "And his anger raged perpetually and he kept his wrath for ever" (Amos 1:11).
   D. R. Simeon b. Laqish said, "His anger and his wrath did not move from his mouth."

Amos attests that Esau held a grudge against his brother Jacob, which his mother could not imagine he would do.

Genesis Rabbah LXVIII:XII.

3. A. Bar Qappara taught on Tannaite authority, "There is no dream without a proper interpretation.
   B. "'That there was a ladder:' refers to the ramp to the altar.
   C. "'...set up on the earth:' that is the altar, 'An altar of dirt you will make for me' (Ex. 20:24).
   D. "'...and the top of it reached to heaven:' these are the offerings, for their fragrance goes up to heaven.
   E. "'...and behold, the angels of God:' these are the high priests.
   F. "'...were ascending and descending on it:' for they go up and go down on the ramp.
   G. "'And behold, the Lord stood above it:' 'I saw the Lord standing by the altar' (Amos 9:1)."

Amos contributes to the interpretation of Jacob's dream. God was standing by the altar that appeared in the dream.

Genesis Rabbah LXX:IV.

2. A. R. Abbahu and rabbis:
   B. R. Abbahu said, "'If God will be with me and will keep me in '*this way*' refers to protection from gossip, in line with this usage: 'And they turn their tongue in the way of slander their bow of falsehood' (Jer. 9:2).
   C. "'...will give me bread to eat' refers to protection from fornication, in line with this usage: 'Neither has he kept back any thing from me, except the bread which he ate' (Gen. 39:9), a euphemism for sexual relations with his wife.
   D. "'...so that I come again to my father's house in peace' refers to bloodshed.
   E. "'...then the Lord shall be my God' so that I shall be protected from idolatry.'"
   F. Rabbis interpreted the statement "*this way*" to speak of all of these.

G. [The rabbis' statement now follows:] "Specifically: 'If God will be with me and will keep me in this way that I go' [by referring only to 'way'] contains an allusion to idolatry, fornication, murder, and slander.

H. "'Way' refers to idolatry: 'They who swear by the sin of Samaria and say, As your god, O Dan, lives, and as the way of Beer sheba lives' (Amos 8:14).

I. "'Way' refers to adultery: 'So is the way of an adulterous woman' (Prov. 30:20).

J. "'Way' refers to murder: 'My son, do not walk in the way of them, restrain your foot from their path, for their feet run to evil and they make haste to shed blood' (Prov. 1:15-16).

K. "'Way' refers to slander: 'And he heard the words of Laban's sons, saying, "Jacob has taken away"' (Gen. 31:1)."

Amos proves that "way" refers to idolatry.

Genesis Rabbah LXXI:II.

7. A. Said R. Samuel bar Nahman, "Since the story is told in connection with Rachel, Israel bears her name, as it is said, 'Rachel is weeping for her children' (Jer. 31:15).

B. "And it is not only in connection with her name, but also in connection with her son's name that Israel is so called: 'It may be that the Lord, the God of hosts, will be gracious to the remnant of Joseph' (Amos 5:15).

C. "And it is not only in connection with her son's name, but also in connection with her grandson's name that Israel is so called: 'Is Ephraim a darling son to me?' (Jer. 31:20)."

Amos speaks of Israel in the name of Joseph.

Genesis Rabbah XCIII:V.

1. A. "Behold the days come, says the Lord, that the plowman will overtake the reaper, and the treader of grapes him who sows seed. And the mountains shall drop sweet wine...." (Amos 9:13):

B. "The days come says the Lord, that the plowman will overtake" refers to Judah.

C. "The reaper" speaks of Joseph: "For behold, we were binding sheaves" (Gen. 37:7).

D. "...and the treader of grapes:" this is Judah: "For I have trodden Judah for me" (Zech. 9:13).

E. "...him who sows seed:" this is Joseph, who sowed the seed of his father and brought them down to Egypt.

F. "...And the mountains shall drop sweet wine:" refers to the tribal progenitors, who said, "If kings contend with one another, what difference does it make to us? It is appropriate for a king to contend

4. *Amos in Genesis Rabbah, Leviticus Rabbah, and Pesiqta deRab Kahana*

with another king [Judah, the founder of Israelite royalty, with the king of Egypt]."

G. "Then Judah went up to him and said, 'O my lord, let your servant, I pray you, speak a word in my lord's ears, and let not your anger burn against your servant, for you are like Pharaoh himself'" (Gen. 44:18).

Amos refers to Judah and Joseph in his prophecy of Amos 9:13.

Genesis Rabbah XCIX:II.

1. A. "For the Lord God will do nothing unless he reveals his secret to his servants the prophets" (Amos 3:7).
   B. Jacob linked two of his sons, corresponding to two of the monarchies, and Moses linked two of the tribes, corresponding to two of the monarchies.
   C. Judah corresponds to the kingdom of Babylonia, for this is compared to a lion and that is compared to a lion. This is compared to a lion: "Judah is a lion's whelp" (Gen. 49:9), and so too Babylonia: "The first was like a lion" (Dan. 7:4).
   D. Then by the hand of which of the tribes will the kingdom of Babylonia fall? It will be by the hand of Daniel, who comes from the tribe of Judah.
   E. Benjamin corresponds to the kingdom of Media, for this is compared to a wolf and that is compared to a wolf. This is compared to a wolf: "Benjamin is a ravenous wolf, [in the morning devouring the prey, and at even dividing the spoil]." And that is compared to a wolf: "And behold, another beast, a second, like a wolf" (Dan. 7:5).
   F. R. Hanina said, "The word for 'wolf' in the latter verse is written as 'bear.' It had been called a bear."
   G. That is the view of R. Yohanan, for R. Yohanan said, "'Wherefore a lion of the forest slays them' (Jer. 5:6) refers to Babylonia, and 'a wolf of the deserts spoils them' refers to Media."
   H. [Reverting to E:] Then by the hand of which of the tribes will the kingdom of Media fall? It will be by the hand of Mordecai, who comes from the tribe of Benjamin.
   I. Levi corresponds to the kingdom of Greece. This is the third tribe in order, and that is the third kingdom in order. This is written with a word that is made up of three letters, and that is written with a word which consists of three letters. This one sounds the horn and that one sounds the horn, this one wears turbans and that one wears helmets, this one wears pants and that one wears knee-cuts.
   J. To be sure, this one is very populous, while that one is few in numbers. But the many came and fell into the hand of the few.
   K. On account of merit deriving from what source did this take place? It is on account of the blessing that Moses bestowed: "Smite through the loins of them that rise up against him" (Deut. 33:11).

L. Then by the hand of which of the tribes will the kingdom of Greece fall? It will be by the hand of sons of the Hasmoneans, who come from the tribe of Levi.'

M. Joseph corresponds to the kingdom of Edom [Rome], for this one has horns and that one has horns. This one has horns: "His firstling bullock, majesty is his, and his horns are the horns of the wild ox" (Deut. 33:17). And that one has horns: "And concerning the ten horns that were on its head" (Dan. 7:20). This one kept away from fornication while that one cleaved to fornication. This one paid respect for the honor owing to his father, while that one despised the honor owing to his father. Concerning this one it is written, "For I fear God" (Gen. 42:18), while in regard to that one it is written, "And he did not fear God" (Deut. 25:18). [So the correspondence in part is one of opposites.]

N. Then by the hand of which of the tribes will the kingdom of Edom fall? It will be by the hand of the anointed for war, who comes from the tribe of Joseph.

O. R. Phineas in the name of R. Samuel b. Nahman: "There is a tradition that Esau will fall only by the hand of the sons of Rachel: 'Surely the least of the flock shall drag them away' (Jer. 49:20). Why the least? Because they are the youngest of the tribes."

The prophet is told God's plan, and Jacob predicted his sons' future. But that is only a general introduction; the details do not derive from Amos.

Genesis Rabbah C:VII.

1. A. "When they came to the threshing floor of Atad, which is beyond the Jordan, they lamented there with a very great and sorrowful lamentation, and he made a mourning for his father seven days" (Gen. 50:10):

B. How on the basis of Scripture do we know that mourning lasts for seven days?

C. R. Aha derives proof from the following: "...and he made a mourning for his father seven days" (Gen. 50:10).

D. But does proof derive from a matter pertaining to the age prior to the giving of the Torah?

E. R. Simeon b. Laqish in the name of Bar Qappara derives proof from the following: "And you shall not go out from the door of the tent of meeting for seven days' (Lev. 8:13). Just as you are anointed with anointing oil for seven days, so you will observe for your brothers seven days [of mourning]."

F. R. Hoshaiah derives proof from the following: "'And at the door of the tent of meeting you shall dwell day and night for seven days and keep the observance of the Lord' (Lev. 8:35). Just as the Holy One, blessed be he, kept an observance for his world for seven days, so you must observe seven days of mourning for your brothers."

4. Amos in Genesis Rabbah, Leviticus Rabbah, and Pesiqta deRab Kahana

G. For R. Joshua b. Levi said, "For seven days the Holy One, blessed be he, went into mourning for his world [before he brought the flood, as it is said, 'And it grieved him in his heart' (Gen. 6:5), and further it says, 'For the king grieved for his son' (2 Sam. 19:3)]."

H. R. Yohanan derives proof from the following: "'Let her not, I pray you, be as one dead,' but rather: 'let her be shut up seven days' (Num. 12:12, 14). Just as the days of shutting up last for a week, so the mourning lasts for seven days."

I. One of the masters told this statement of R. Yohanan to R. Simeon b. Laqish, who did not accept it. Why did he not accept it? He said, "[Freedman:] There the rule treats the case as a matter of shutting up, while here it is treated as a matter of decided and definite illness."

J. R. Abbahu in the name of R. Yohanan came and said, "'Let her not, I pray you, be as one dead,' (Num. 12:12, 14). Just as the days of mourning for the deceased last for a week, so the period of probationary waiting lasts for seven days."

K. Said R. Jeremiah and R. Hiyya bar Abba in the name of R. Simeon b. Laqish, "'And I will turn your feasts into mourning' (Amos 8:10).

L. "Just as the days of the Festival [of Tabernacles] are seven, so the period of mourning should be seven days."

See Yerushalmi Moed Qatan 3:3 I:13.

LEVITICUS RABBAH

Leviticus Rabbah V:I

1. A. "If it is the anointed priest who sins, [thus bringing guilt on the people, then let him offer to the Lord for the sin which he has committed a young bull without blemish]" (Lev. 4:3).

B. "When he is quiet, who can condemn? When he hides his face, who can set him right [RSV: behold him] [whether it be a nation or a man? that a godless man should not reign, that he should not ensnare the people]" (Job 34:29-30).

Leviticus Rabbah V:III

1. A. Another interpretation of "When he is quiet, who can condemn? When he hides his face, who can set him right?" (Job 34:29).

B. When he gave tranquillity to the ten tribes, who could come and condemn them?

C. What sort of tranquillity did he give them? "Woe to those who are at ease in Zion, and to those who feel secure on the mountain of Samaria, the notable men of the first of the nations, to whom the house of Israel to come" (Amos 6:1).

Amos illustrates the point of Job 34:29, that when things are prosperous, the people rebel.

Leviticus Rabbah V:III

3. A. "Pass over to Calneh and see, [and thence go to Hamath the great, then go down to Gath of the Philistines. Are they better than these kingdoms? Or is their territory greater than your territory?]" (Amos 6:2).
   B. [Calneh] refers to Ctesiphon.
   C. "Hamath the great" refers to Hamath of Antioch.
   D. "And go down to Gath of the Philistines" refers to the mounds of the Philistines.
   E. "Are they better than these kingdoms? Or is their territory greater than your territory?"
   F. "O you who put far away the evil day" (Amos 6:3) [refers to] the day on which they would go into exile.
4. A. "And bring near the seat of violence?" (Amos 6:3). This refers to Esau.
   B. "Did you bring yourselves near to sit next to violence" — this refers to Esau.
   C. That is in line with the following verse of Scripture: "For the violence done to your brother Jacob, [shame shall cover you]" (Obad. 1:40).
5. A. "[Woe to] those who lie upon beds of ivory" (Amos 6:4) — on beds made of the elephant's tusk.
   B. "And stink on their couches" (Amos 6:4) — who do stinking transgressions on their beds.
   C. "Who eat lambs from the flock [and calves from the midst of the stall]" (Amos 6:4).
   D. They say: When one of them wanted to eat a kid of the flock, he would have the whole flock brought before him, and he would stand over it and slaughter it.
   E. When he wanted to eat a calf, he would bring the entire herd of calves before him and stand over it and slaughter it.
6. A. "Who sing idle songs to the sound of the harp [and like David invent for themselves instruments of music]" (Amos 6:5).
   B. [They would say that] David provided them with musical instruments.
7. A. "Who drink wine in bowls" (Amos 6:6).
   B. Rab, R. Yohanan, and rabbis:
   C. Rab said, "It is a very large bowl" [using the Greek].
   D. R. Yohanan said, "It was in small cups."
   E. Rabbis say, "It was in cups with saucers attached."
   F. Whence did the wine they drink come?
   G. R. Aibu in the name of R. Hanina said, "It was wine from Pelugta, for the wine would entice (PTH) the body."
   H. And rabbis in the name of R. Hanina said, "It was from Pelugta's [separation], since, because of their wine drinking, the ten tribes were enticed [from God] and consequently sent into exile."
8. A. "And anoint themselves with the finest oils" (Amos 6:6).

4. Amos in Genesis Rabbah, Leviticus Rabbah, and Pesiqta deRab Kahana

B. R. Judah b. R. Ezekiel said, "This refers to oil of unripe olives, which removes hair and smooths the body."
C. R. Haninah said, "This refers to oil of myrrh and cinnamon."
9. A. And [in spite of] all this glory: "They are not grieved over the ruin of Joseph" (Amos 6:6).
B. "Therefore they shall now be the first of those to go into exile, [and the revelry of those who stretch themselves shall pass away]" (Amos 6:7).
C. What is the meaning of "the revelry of those who stretch themselves"?
D. Said R. Aibu, "They had thirteen public baths, one for each of the tribes, and one additional one for all of them together.
E. "And all of them were destroyed, and only this one [that had served all of them] survived.
F. "This shows how much lewdness was done with them."

We find a systematic exegesis of Amos 6:2-6. Amos speaks of Ctesiphon and Hamath and other kingdoms that went into exile. At No. 4 he speaks of Rome/Esau. No. 5 speaks of the conspicuous waste of the Israelites. The following compositions gloss the language of the prophet.

Leviticus Rabbah VI:VI

1. A. [With reference to Is. 8:18-19: "Behold, I and the children whom the Lord has given me are signs and portents in Israel from the Lord of hosts, who dwells on Mount Zion. And when they say to you, 'Consult the mediums and the wizards who chirp and mutter,' should not a people consult their God? Should they consult the dead on behalf of the living?"] said R. Simeon, "Two verses [only] did Beeri [father of Hosea, Hos. 1:1] prophesy, and they were not enough to fill a scroll, so they are attached to the book of Isaiah.
B. "And these are they: 'And when they say to you, Consult the mediums and the wizards' [Is. 8:19] and the neighboring verse" (8:20).
2. A. Said R. Yohanan, "Every prophet, whose name and the name of whose father is made explicit, is a prophet son of a prophet. And anyone whose name is given, while the name of his father is not given, is a prophet but not the son of a prophet."
B. R. Eleazar in the name of R. Yosé b. Zimra said, "It is written, 'And Haggai, the prophet, and Zechariah son of Iddo the prophet prophesied' [Ezra 5:1], so the latter was a prophet son of a prophet.
C. "One verse of Scripture says, 'Isaiah son of Amoz, the prophet' [2 Kgs. 20:1], and another verse of Scripture says, 'Isaiah the prophet, son of Amoz' [2 Kgs. 19:2]. This indicates that he was a prophet, son of a prophet."
D. [Responding to Yohanan's thesis, above, A], rabbis say, "Whether his [father's] name is or is not made explicit, he still is a prophet son of a prophet.

E. "For note, Amos says to Amaziah, 'I am not a prophet nor the son of a prophet' [Amos 7:14]. Just as he really was a prophet, but said, 'I am not a prophet,' so too his father really was a prophet, but he said of him that his father was not a prophet."

Amos illustrates Yohanan's dictum concerning the denial of prophecy.

Leviticus Rabbah VII:I

1. A. "[The Lord said to Moses,] 'Command Aaron [and his sons, saying, This is the law of the burnt offering']" (Lev. 6:2 [RSV: 6:9]).
   B. "Hatred stirs up strife, but love covers all offenses" (Prov. 10:12).
2. A. Another interpretation: "Hatred stirs up strife" (Prov. 10:12).
   B. [This refers to] the hatred which Aaron brought between Israel and their father in heaven.
   C. "Stirs up strife" (MDNYM) — provoked judgments.
   D. Said R. Assi, "[Scripture] teaches that [Aaron] took a hammer and battered [the golden calf] before [the people], saying to them, 'See, there really is nothing in it.'
   E. "That is what the Holy One, blessed be he, told Moses: 'Him who has sinned against me shall I wipe out from my book' [Ex. 32:33].
   F. "That is in line with the following verse of Scripture: 'Moreover the Lord was very angry with Aaron, such as to destroy him'" (Deut. 9:20).
   G. Said R. Joshua of Sikhnin in the name of R. Levi, "The word, 'destroy,' used here means only the extinction of sons and daughters.
   H. "That is in line with the use of the same word in the following verse: 'And I destroyed his fruit from above and his root from beneath' [Amos 2:9].
   I. "'But love covers all offenses' [Prov. 10:12]. [This refers to] the prayer that Moses said in [Aaron's] behalf [for he did have sons]."
   J. What prayer did he say in his behalf?
   K. R. Mana of Sha'ab and R. Joshua of Sikhnin in the name of R. Levi: "From the beginning of the scroll [of Leviticus] to this point, it is written, 'And the sons of Aaron will offer' [Lev. 1:5], 'The sons of Aaron will place . . . ' [Lev. 1:7], 'The sons of Aaron will arrange' [Lev. 1:8], 'The sons of Aaron will burn' [Lev. 3:5].
   L. "Said Moses before the Holy One, blessed be he, 'Lord of the world, will the well be hated but its waters precious?
   M. "'You paid respect to trees because of their offspring [which would be valuable in the agricultural life of the Holy Land],'
   N. "as we have learned in the Mishnah: '**All trees may be used for burning on the altar fire except the olive tree and the vine [which are too valuable for that purpose]**' [M. Tam. 2:3].
   O. "'Will you not pay any honor at all to Aaron on account of his offspring?'

4. Amos in Genesis Rabbah, Leviticus Rabbah, and Pesiqta deRab Kahana

P. "Said to him the Holy One, blessed be he, 'By your life, on account of your prayer I shall bring him back, and not only so, but I shall make him the main act and his sons the sideshow': 'Command Aaron and his sons, saying'" (Lev. 6:2).

Amos's usage of the word "destroy" speaks of the loss of children.

Leviticus Rabbah X:II

1. A. R. Azariah in the name of R. Judah b. R. Simon interpreted the verse ["You love righteousness and hate wickedness, therefore God, your God, has anointed you with the oil of gladness above your fellows" (Ps. 45:7)] to speak of Isaiah:
   B. "Said Isaiah, 'I was strolling in my study house, and I heard the voice of the Holy One [blessed be he] saying, "Whom shall I send? And who will go for us" (Is. 6:8).
   C. "'"When I sent Micah, they hit him on the cheek."'
   D. "That is in line with the following verse of Scripture: 'They smite the judge of Israel with a rod upon the cheek' (Mic. 4:14).
   E. "'"When I sent Amos, they called him the stammerer."'
   F. "[Isaiah] said, 'The Holy One, blessed be he, had no one better upon whom to cause his Presence to rest than that tongue-tied stammerer!'"
   G. Said R. Phineas, "Why was he called Amos? Because his tongue was heavy-laden (amus)."
   H. "'"Whom shall I send, and who will go for us?"'
   I. "Forthwith: 'And I said, Here am I! Send me!' [Is. 6:8].

Amos was an example of the messengers whom God sent, a stammerer.

Leviticus Rabbah X:V

7. A. In the view of R. Joshua b. Levi, who has said that prayer only accomplishes part of the required atonement, from whom do you derive proof?
   B. It is from Aaron, against whom a decree was issued.
   C. That is in line with the following verse: "Moreover the Lord was very angry with Aaron, to have destroyed him" (Deut. 9:20).
   D. R. Joshua of Sikhnin said in the name of R. Levi, "The meaning of the word 'destruction' used here is only the utter extinction of all offspring, sons and daughters alike.
   E. "That is in line with the following usage: 'And I destroyed his fruit from above and his roots from beneath'" (Amos 2:9).
   F. Yet when Moses prayed on behalf of Aaron, only two of his sons died [Nadab and Abihu], while the other two survived.
   G. "Take Aaron and his sons with him" (Lev. 8:2).

As above.

Leviticus Rabbah XII:I

1. A. "[And the Lord spoke to Aaron, saying,] 'Drink no wine nor strong drink, [you nor your sons with you, when you go into the tent of meeting, lest you die; it shall be a statute forever throughout your generations]'" (Lev. 10:9).
12. A. Another interpretation: "It stings like an adder" (Prov. 23:32).
    B. Just as an adder distinguishes between death and life, so did wine cause a separation between the ten tribes in the matter of the exile.
    C. That is in line with what is written: "Woe to those who rise early in the morning, that they may run after strong drink, who tarry late in the evening till wine inflames them" (Is. 5:11).
    D. "... who drink wine in bowls ... " (Amos 6:6).
    E. On this account: "Therefore they shall now be the first of those who go into exile" (Amos 6:7).

Those who misuse wine go into exile.

Leviticus Rabbah XVII:IV

1. A. R. Huniah in the name of R. Joshua b. R. Abin and R. Zechariah, son-in-law of R. Levi, in the name of R. Levi: "The merciful Lord does not do injury to human beings first. [First he exacts a penalty from property, aiming at the sinner's repentance.]
   B. "From whom do you derive that lesson? From the case of Job: 'The oxen were plowing and the asses feeding beside them; [and the Sabeans fell upon them and took them and slew the servants with the edge of the sword; and I alone have escaped to tell you' (Job 1:14). Afterward: 'Your sons and daughters were eating and drinking wine in their eldest brother's house, and behold, a great wind came across the wilderness and struck the four corners of the house, and it fell upon the young people, and they are dead' (Job 1:19).]"
   C. Now were the oxen plowing, and the asses feeding beside them?
   D. Said R. Hama b. R. Hanina, "This teaches that the Holy One, blessed be he, showed him a paradigm of the world to come.
   E. "That is in line with the following verse of Scripture: 'The plowman shall overtake the reaper'" (Amos 9:13).

In the world to come, Amos says, the plowman will overtake the reaper.

Leviticus Rabbah XIX:IV

1. A. R. Kohen opened [discourse by citing the following verse]: "'Through sloth [restraint] the roof sinks in, [and through indolence the house leaks]' (Qoh. 10:18).
2. E. "The house leaks": "For behold, the Lord has commanded, and the great house will be smitten into splinters, and the small house into chips" (Amos 6:11).

F. The two [the great house: the kingdom of Israel, the ten tribes, and the small house: Judah] are not equivalent to one another. [The great house was demolished, the small one merely damaged.]

Amos refers the "house" of the cited verse to the ten tribes and the two tribes.

Leviticus Rabbah XX:VI

1. A. R. Berekhiah opened [discourse by citing the following verse of Scripture: "'To impose a fine on a righteous man is not good; [to flog noble men for the sake of uprightness]' [Prov. 17:26].
   B. "Said the Holy One, blessed be he, 'Even though I punished Aaron and took his two sons from him, it is not good.' But it was 'to flog noble men for the sake of uprightness'" (Prov. 17:26).
   C. "After the death of the two sons of Aaron" (Lev. 16:2).
2. A. It was taught in the name of R. Eliezer: "Nadab and Abihu died only because they gave instruction in the presence of Moses, their master."
   B. There was the case of a disciple who gave instruction in the presence of his master, R. Eliezer. He said to Imma Shalom, his wife, "He is not going to live out the week." The Sabbath had not come before he died.
   C. His students came and said to him, "Rabbi, are you then a prophet?"
   D. He said to them, "'I am not a prophet nor the disciple of a prophet' (Amos 7:14), but this is the tradition which I have received: 'Any [disciple] who teaches a law in his master's presence is liable to the death penalty.'"

Amos is cited by Eliezer.

Leviticus Rabbah XXVI:VII

3. A. Rabbi would explain the meaning of verses of Scripture. When he came to these verses, he would weep:
   B. "For lo, he who forms the mountains and creates the wind and tells a man his thought" (Amos 4:14). Even things that have no substance whatsoever are written down in a person's record in his notebook.
   C. Who writes them down? "He who makes the morning gloom" (Amos 4:13).
   D. And this verse also: "Seek the Lord, all you humble of the earth, seek righteousness, seek humility, perhaps you will be hidden on the day of the wrath of the Lord" (Zeph. 2:3).
   E. And this verse also: "Hate evil, love good, establish justice in the gate, perhaps the Lord of hosts will show you grace, O remnant of Joseph" (Amos 5:15).
   F. And this verse also: "For God will bring every evil deed unto judgment" (Qoh. 12:14).

G. And this verse also: "Let him put his mouth in the dust, perhaps there may be hope" (Lam. 3:29).
H. And this verse also: "Then Samuel said to Saul, Why have you disturbed me" (1 Sam. 28:15).
I. He said to him, "You should have not disturbed your Creator, but rather me. You have made an idol of me.
J. "Did you not know that just as they exact punishment from the one who worships [an idol], so they exact punishment from the one who is worshipped as an idol?
K. "And not only so, but since I thought that it was the Day of Judgment, I brought Moses along with me!"
L. Now is it not an argument a fortiori: If Samuel, the master of the prophets, concerning whom it was written, "Samuel was established to be a prophet of the Lord" (1 Sam. 3:20), was afraid of the day of judgment, all other people all the more so [should be afraid of it]!

Amos says that God records whatever one thinks, not only what he does.

Leviticus Rabbah XXX:XII

1. A. Another interpretation: "The fruit of goodly trees" refers to Israel.
   B. Just as a citron has both taste and fragrance, so in Israel are people who have [the merit of both] Torah and good deeds.
   C. "Branches of palm trees" (Lev. 23:30): refers to Israel. Just as a palm has a taste but no fragrance, so in Israel are people who have [the merit of] Torah but not of good deeds.
   D. "Boughs of leafy trees:" refers to Israel. Just as a myrtle has a fragrance but no taste, so in Israel are people who have the merit of good deeds but not of Torah.
   E. "Willows of the brook:" refers to Israel. Just as a willow has neither taste nor fragrance, so in Israel are those who have the [merit] neither of Torah nor of good deeds.
   F. What does the Holy One, blessed be he, do for them? Utterly to destroy them is not possible.
   G. Rather, said the Holy One, blessed be he, "Let them all be joined together in a single bond, and they will effect atonement for one another.
   H. "And if you have done so, at that moment I shall be exalted."
   I. That is in line with the following verse of Scripture: "He who builds his upper chambers in heaven" (Amos 9:6).
   J. And when is he exalted? When they are joined together in a single bond, as it is said, "When he has founded his bond upon the earth" (Amos 9:6).
   K. Therefore Moses admonishes Israel: "And you shall take . . . " (Lev. 23:40).

The Israelites are embodied in the fruit of goodly trees. He joins them all together in a single bond and they support one another. That is when God is exalted in heaven.

Leviticus Rabbah XXIII:II

1. A. "He showed me: behold, the Lord was standing beside a wall built with a plumb line (NK) [with a plumb line in his hand]" (Amos 7:7).
   B. [He was standing] beside a wall of wrongs. [The Hebrew, NK, in Aramaic is translated "wrong."]
2. A. "And in his hand was a plumb line" (Amos 7:7).
   B. He was like a creditor who was standing with the bond [of debt] in his hand.
   C. Along these same lines: "A new king arose" (Ex. 1:8).
   D. He was like a creditor who was standing with the bond in his hand.
   E. Along these same lines: "And the seven years of famine arose" (Gen. 41:30).
   F. It was like a creditor who was standing with the bond in his hand.
   G. And along these same lines: "And Balak son of Zippor saw" (Num. 22:2).
   H. He was like a creditor who was standing with the bond in his hand.
   I. And along these same lines: "[You saw, O king, and behold,] a great image. This image, mighty [and of exceeding brightness, stood before you]" (Dan. 7:31).
   J. It was like a creditor who was standing with the bond in his hand. [In each case, the "creditor" is standing and waiting to exact collection of what is owing to him.]
3. A. "And the Lord said to me, 'Amos, what do you see' And I said, 'A plumb line'" (Amos 7:8).
   B. What is the meaning of the word for plumb line (NK)?
   C. This refers to the great Sanhedrin of Israel, which adds up to the number [of seventy-one, the same as the numerical value of the letters of the word] NK.
4. A. "And the Lord said, 'Behold, I am setting a plumb line [in the midst of my people Israel]'" (Amos 7:8).
   B. Said R. Judah bar Simon, "Just as a pot on the fire does not hold its weight but diminishes (NKH) [through the fire's action], so the Holy One, blessed be he, said, 'I shall diminish you through suffering in this world, but in the world to come: "I will not continue to be angry with them any longer"'" (Amos 7:8).
5. A. R. Isaac bar Eleazar and R. Tabyomi in the name of R. Jeremiah, R. Berekhiah in the name of R. Eleazar: "In regard to all other transgressions, it is written, 'Forgiving iniquity and transgression' (Ex. 34:7).
   B. "But in this case [when it speaks of hurting another party through words], 'I shall not continue to pardon'" (Amos 7:8).

Amos 7:7-8 is subjected to a phrase by phrase exegesis. No. 1 moralizes the vision of God standing beside a well built wall. It is a wall of wrongs, and God checks the wall with a plumb line. The Israelites suffer in this world but will not be punished in the world to come, No. 4, and God forgives all manner of transgression except for injury done through words,

Leviticus Rabbah XXXIII:III

1. A. "I saw the Lord standing over the altar (MZBH)" (Amos 9:1).
   B. He was standing over that generation, to slay it (ZBH).
   C. "And he said, 'Smite the capitals'" (Amos 9:1). This refers to Josiah, king of Judah.
   D. "Until the thresholds shake" (Amos 9:1). This refers to his counselors.
2. A. "And shatter them (BSM) on the heads of all the people" (Amos 9:1).
   B. R. Simeon bar Abba in the name of R. Yohanan: "Their [acts of] robbery (BSM) are at the head of all [their sins, and so] stand out most of all."
   C. R. Yudan in the name of R. Yohanan: "The matter may be compared to a basket full of sins. Which among them draws the strongest indictment? It is thievery."
   D. R. Phineas in the name of R. Yohanan: "The matter may be compared to a group of people, among whom were idolators, murderers, fornicators. But the act of thievery [of which] all of them [were guilty] was the most weighty of all [of their sins]."
   E. Said R. Jacob bar Aha in the name of R. Yohanan, "Ezekiel made a list of twenty-four sins, and among them all, he concluded [the list] only with robbery: 'Behold, therefore, I have smitten my hand on your acts of robbery (BSK)'" (Ez. 22:13).
   F. Therefore Moses admonishes Israel, saying to them, "You shall not wrong one another" (Lev. 25:14).

Amos 9:1 is given a phrase by phrase exegesis.

PESIQTA DERAB KAHANA

Pesiqta deRab Kahana III:I

1. A. "Remember [what the Amalekites did to you on your way out of Egypt, how they met you on the road when you were faint and weary and cut off your rear, which was lagging behind exhausted; they showed no fear of God. When the Lord your God gives you peace from your enemies on every side, in the land which he is giving you to occupy as your patrimony, you shall not fail to blot out the memory of the Amalekites from under heaven]" (Deut. 25:17-19).

4. Amos in Genesis Rabbah, Leviticus Rabbah, and Pesiqta deRab Kahana

2. A. What was the sin that he committed against his mother [to whom reference is made in the intersecting-verse, ...and his mother's wickedness never be wiped out]?
   B. R. Tanhum bar Abun and R. Judah and R. Nehemiah and rabbis:
   C. R. Judah says, "When he was coming out of his mother's womb, he cut off her uterus, so that she should not give birth again. That is in line with this verse of Scripture, 'Because he pursued his brother with a sword, he destroyed the womb whence he came' (Amos 1:11)."
   D. Said R. Berekhiah, "You should not conclude that it was merely [adventitious, that is,] because he was coming forth from his mother's womb, but as he was coming out of his mother's womb, his fist was [deliberately] stretched out toward [his brother, and this was intentional]. What verse of Scripture so indicates? 'The wicked have a fist from the womb, liars go astray as soon as they are born' (Ps. 58:4)."
   E. R. Nehemiah says, "He caused her not to produce the twelve tribes."
   F. For R. Huna said, "Rebecca was worthy of producing all the twelve tribes, a fact indicated by this verse:' And the Lord said to her, Two nations are in your womb' (Gen. 25:23). Lo, there are two. 'And two peoples will separate from your belly' (Gen. 25:23), thus four.' One people shall be stronger than the other' — so six; 'the elder shall serve the younger' — eight; 'And when her days to be delivered were fulfilled, behold there were twins in her womb,' then ten; 'And the first came forth and after that came forth his brother.. '.– twelve in all."
   G. There are those who prove the same proposition from this verse of Scripture: 'If this is the way my childbearing is to go, why should I bear this' (Gen. 25:22). The word for this is composed of the letters Z and H, the numerical value of which is seven and five, respectively, thus twelve.
   H. And rabbis say, "[Esau] caused her bier not to be carried out in public. You find that when Rebecca died, people said, 'Who is going to go forth before the bier? Abraham is dead, Isaac is blind and stays at home, Jacob has fled before Esau. Will the wicked Esau be permitted to go forth before her bier?' People will say, 'Cursed be the teats that suckled that one.'
   I. "What did they do? They brought out her bier by night [without public display]."
   J. Said R. Yosé bar Haninah, "And since her bier was not carried out in public, Scripture too dealt with her death only obliquely: Deborah, 'Rebecca's nurse died...and was buried below Beth-el under the oak, which was called Allon-bacuth' [bacuth being understood to mean weeping] (Gen. 35:8)."

Amos condemns Esau for destroying his mother's womb.

Pesiqta deRab Kahana V:IX

13. A. And rabbis say, "In the septennate in which the son of David comes, in the first of the seven year spell, 'I shall cause it to rain on one town and not on another' (Amos 4:7).
   B. "In the second, the arrows of famine will be sent forth.
   C. "In the third there will be a great famine, and men, women, and children will die in it, and the Torah will be forgotten in Israel.
   D. "In the fourth, there will be a famine which is not really a famine, and plenty which is not plentiful.
   E. "In the fifth year, there will be great plenty, and people will eat and drink and rejoice, and the Torah will again be renewed.
   F. "In the sixth there will be great thunders.
   G. "In the seventh there will be wars.
   H. "And at the end of the seventh year of that septennate, the son of David will come."
   I. Said R. Abbayye, "How many septennates have there been like this one, and yet he has not come."

Amos speaks of the seven years in which the son of David comes.

Pesiqta deRab Kahana VII:X

1. A. R. Huna and R. Joshua bar Abin, son-in-law of R. Levi, in the name of R. Levi: "The Merciful God does not touch lives first of all [but exacts vengeance on property]. From whom do you learn that fact? From Job: A messenger came to Job and said, 'The oxen were plowing and the asses feeding beside them' (Job 1:14)."
   B. What is the meaning of," and the asses feeding beside them"?
   C. Said R. Hama, "A model of the order of the world to come was made for him, in line with this verse: 'Behold, the days are coming, says the Lord, when the one who ploughs shall overtake the one who reaps' (Amos 9:13)."

Amos speaks once more of the world to come.

Pesiqta deRab Kahana XIII:XI

2. A. In ten upward stages the Presence of God departed: from the cherub to the cherub, from the cherub to the threshold of the temple-building; from the threshold of the temple to the two cherubim; from the two cherubim to the eastern gate of the sanctuary; from the eastern gate of the sanctuary to the [wall of the] temple court; from the [wall of the] temple court to the altar; from the altar to the roof; from the roof to the city wall, from the city wall to the city, from the city to the Mount of Olives.
   B. ...from the ark cover to the cherub: "And he rode upon a cherub and flew" (2 Sam. 22:11).

4. Amos in Genesis Rabbah, Leviticus Rabbah, and Pesiqta deRab Kahana 57

C. ...from the cherub to the cherub: "And the glory of the Lord mounted up from the cherub to the threshold of the house" (Ez. 10:45).

D. ...from the threshold of the temple to the two cherubim: "And the glory of the Lord went forth from off the threshold of the house and stood over the cherubim" (Ez. 10:18). Lo, it was necessary to say only, "And the glory of the Lord came..."

E. They drew a parable: to what may the matter be compared? To the case of a king who was leaving his palace. He kissed the walls and embraced the columns and said, "May you remain whole, O my house, may you remain whole, O my palace." So the Presence of God kissed the walls and embraced the columns and said, "May you remain whole, O my house, may you remain whole, O my palace."

F. ...from the two cherubim to the eastern gate of the sanctuary: "The cherubs raised their wings and flew above the earth before my eyes" (Ez. 10:9).

G. ...from the eastern gate of the sanctuary to the [wall of the] temple court: "And the courtyard was filled with the splendor of the glory of the Lord" (Ez. 10:4).

H. ...from the [wall of the temple] court to the altar: "I saw the Lord standing beside the altar" (Amos 9:1).

I. ...from the altar to the roof: "It is better to dwell on the corner of the roof" (Prov. 21:9).

J. ...from the roof to the city wall: "Lo, he showed me, and behold, the Lord was standing on the wall made by a plumb line" (Amos 7:7).

K. ...from the city wall to the city: "A voice cries, The Lord into the city" (Mic. 6:9).

L. ...from the city to the Mount of Olives: "And the glory of the Lord went up from the midst of the city and stood on the mountain" (Ez. 11:23).

Amos contributes to the vision of the Presence of God's leaving the Temple when it was destroyed.

Pesiqta deRab Kahana XIII:XV

1. A. "The word of the Lord came to him in the thirteenth year of the reign of Josiah son of Amon, king of Judah; also during the reign of Jehoiakim, son of Josiah, king of Judah, until the eleventh year of Zedekiah son of Josiah, king of Judah, was completed. In the fifth month the people of Jerusalem were carried away into exile" (Jer. 1:1-3):

B. Said R. Abun, "A lion came up under the sign of the lion and destroyed the lion of God [=Ariel] [that is, Jerusalem].

C. "...the lion came up: this is Nebuchadnezzar the wicked, concerning whom it is written, 'The lion has come up out of its thicket' (Jer. 4:7).

D. "...under the sign of the lion: 'In the fifth month the people of Jerusalem were carried away into exile.'

E. "...and destroyed the lion of God: 'Oh, Ariel, Ariel, the city where David encamped' (Is. 29:1).

F. "It was so that the lion should come up in the sign of the lion and rebuild the lion of God [Ariel, Jerusalem].

G. "...the lion should come up: thus is the Holy One, blessed be He, of whom it is written, 'The lion has roared, who will not tremble' (Amos 3:8).

H. "...in the sign of the lion: 'And I shall change their time of mourning to rejoicing' (Jer. 31:13).

I "...and rebuild the lion of God: 'the Lord builds Jerusalem, the scattered ones of Israel he will bring back together' (Ps. 147:2)."

Amos speaks of God's roaring.

Pesiqta deRab Kahana XV:IV

1. A. "Thus says the Lord of hosts: 'Consider, and call for the mourning women to come. [Send for the skilful women to come; let them make haste and raise a wailing over us, that our eyes may run down with tears, and our eyelids gush with water. For a sound of wailing is heard from Zion: 'How we are ruined, we are utterly shamed, because we have left the land, because they have cast down our dwellings]'" (Jer. 9:17-19):

B. R. Yohanan, R. Simeon b. Laqish, and rabbis:

C. R. Yohanan said, "The matter may be compared to the case of a king who had two sons. He got mad at the first and took a staff and beat him and sent him away.

D. "He said, 'Woe is this one! From how abundant a life he has been driven out.'

E. "He got mad at the second and took a staff and beat him and sent him away. He said, 'I am the one whose way of bringing up sons is all wrong.'

F. "So the Ten Tribes went into exile, and the Holy One, blessed be He, thereupon recited in their regard this verse: 'Woe is them, for they have strayed from me' (Hos. 7:13).

G. "But when the tribes of Judah and Benjamin went into exile, it is as if the Holy One, blessed be He, said, 'Woe is me on account of my hurt' (Jer. 10:19)."

2. A. R. Simeon b. Laqish said, "The matter may be compared to the case of a king who had two sons. He got mad at the first and took a staff and beat him, and he gasped and died.

4. Amos in Genesis Rabbah, Leviticus Rabbah, and Pesiqta deRab Kahana

B. "The matter may be compared to the case of a king who had two sons. He got mad at the second and took a staff and beat him, and he gasped and died.

C. "He said, 'I have not got the strength to mourn for him, but call the professional mourning women and have them mourn for him.'

D. "So when the Ten Tribes went into exile, the Holy One, blessed be He, began to mourn for them, reciting this verse: 'Listen to this word, which I raise concerning you as a lamentation' (Amos 5:1).

E. "But when the tribes of Judah and Benjamin went into exile, it is as if the Holy One, blessed be He, said, 'I do not have the strength to mourn for you, but call the professional mourning women and have them mourn for them.'

F. "That is in line with this verse of Scripture: 'Thus says the Lord of hosts: 'Consider, and call for the mourning women to come. Send for the skilful women to come; let them make haste and raise a wailing over us, that our eyes may run down with tears, and our eyelids gush with water. For a sound of wailing is heard from Zion: 'How we are ruined, we are utterly shamed, because we have left the land, because they have cast down our dwellings' (Jer. 9:17-19).""

Amos sets forth God's lament at the exile of the ten northern tribes.

Pesiqta deRab Kahana XVI:IV

1. A. "You have loved right and hated wrong; so God, your God, has anointed you above your fellows with oil, the token of joy" (Ps. 45:8):

2. A. R. Azariah in the name of R. Judah bar Simon interpreted the verse to speak of Isaiah:

B. "Said Isaiah, 'I was strolling in my study house, and I heard the voice of the Lord, saying, Whom shall I send? And who will go for us? (Is. 6:8).

C. "He said, 'I sent Amos, and they called him the stammerer.'"

D. Said R. Phineas, "Why was he called Amos? Because [his tongue was heave-laden (amus)] and so he was a stammerer."

E. They said, "The Holy One, blessed be He, dismissed his entire world and brought his Presence to rest only on this stammerer, him of the cut-off tongue."

F. [Resuming discourse broken off at C:] "'When I sent Micah, they hit him on the cheek.' They smite the judge of Israel with a rod upon the cheek (Mic. 4:14).

G. "Now: whom shall I send, And who will go for us (Is. 6:8)?'

H. "Forthwith: 'Here am I, send me'" (Is. 6:8).

Amos was a damaged messenger of God.

Pesiqta deRab Kahana XVI:VIII

1. A. "How will you comfort me through vanity, and as for your answers, there remains only faithlessness" (Job 21:34):
   B. Said R. Abba bar Kahana [on the meaning of the word translated as faithlessness], "Your words [of comfort and consolation, that Job's friends had provided him] require clarification."
   C. Rabbis say, "Your words contain contradictions." [We shall now have a long series of examples of how God's messages to the prophets contradict themselves.]
2. A. The Holy One said to the prophets, "Go and comfort Jerusalem."
   B. Hosea went to give comfort. He said to her [the city], "The Holy One, blessed be He, has sent me to you to bring you comfort."
   C. She said to him, "What do you have in hand."
   D. He said to her, 'I will be as the dew to Israel' (Hos. 14:6).
   E. She said to him, "Yesterday, you said to me, 'Ephraim is smitten, their root is dried up, they shall bear no fruit' (Hos. 9:16), and now you say this to me? Which shall we believe, the first statement or the second?"
3. A. Joel went to give comfort. He said to the city, "The Holy One, blessed be He, has sent me to you to bring you comfort."
   C. She said to him, "What do you have in hand."
   D. He said to her, It shall come to pass in that day that the mountains shall drop down sweet wine and the hills shall flow with milk' (Joel 4:18).
   E. She said to him, "Yesterday, you said to me, 'Awake you drunkards and weep, wail, you who drink wine, because of the sweet wine, for it is cut off from your mouth' (Joel 1:5), and now you say this to me? Which shall we believe, the first statement or the second?"
4. A. Amos went to give comfort. He said to the city, "The Holy One, blessed be He, has sent me to you to bring you comfort."
   C. She said to him, "What do you have in hand."
   D. He said to her, 'On that day I will raise up the fallen tabernacle of David' (Amos 9:11).
   E. She said to him, "Yesterday, you said to me, 'The virgin of Israel is fallen, she shall no more rise' (Amos 5:2), and now you say this to me? Which shall we believe, the first statement or the second?"
5. A. Micah went to give comfort. He said to the city, "The Holy One, blessed be He, has sent me to you to bring you comfort."
   C. She said to him, "What do you have in hand."
   D. He said to her, "Who is like God to you who pardons iniquity and passes by transgression" (Mic. 7:18).
   E. She said to him, "Yesterday, you said to me, 'For the transgression of Jacob is all this and for the sins of the house of Israel' (Mic. 1:56), and now you say this to me? Which shall we believe, the first statement or the second?"
6. A. Nahum went to give comfort. He said to the city, "The Holy One, blessed be He, has sent me to you to bring you comfort."

4. Amos in Genesis Rabbah, Leviticus Rabbah, and Pesiqta deRab Kahana

- C. She said to him, "What do you have in hand."
- D. He said to her, "The wicked one shall no more pass through you, he is utterly cut off" (Nahum 2:1).
- E. She said to him, "Yesterday, you said to me,' Out of you came he forth who devises evil against the Lord, who counsels wickedness' (Nah. 1:11), and now you say this to me? Which shall we believe, the first statement or the second?"

7. A. Habakkuk went to give comfort. He said to the city, "The Holy One, blessed be He, has sent me to you to bring you comfort."
- C. She said to him, "What do you have in hand."
- D. He said to her, ""You have come forth for the deliverance of your people, for the deliverance of your anointed" (Hab. 3:13).
- E. She said to him, "Yesterday, you said to me, How long, O Lord, shall I cry and you will not hear, "I cry to you of violence" (Hab. 1:22), and now you say this to me? Which shall we believe, the first statement or the second?"

8. A. Zephaniah went to give comfort. He said to the city, "The Holy One, blessed be He, has sent me to you to bring you comfort."
- C. She said to him, "What do you have in hand."
- D. He said to her, "It shall come to pass at that time that I will search Jerusalem with the lamps" (Zeph. 1:12).
- E. She said to him, "Yesterday, you said to me, 'A day of darkness and gloominess a day of clouds and thick darkness' (Zeph. 1:15), and now you say this to me? Which shall we believe, the first statement or the second?"

9. A. Haggai went to give comfort. He said to the city, "The Holy One, blessed be He, has sent me to you to bring you comfort."
- C. She said to him, "What do you have in hand."
- D. He said to her, "Shall the seed ever again remain in the barn? Shall the vine, the fig tree, the pomegranate, and the olive tree ever again bear no fruit? Indeed not, from this day I will bless you" (Hag. 2:19).
- E. She said to him, "Yesterday, you said to me, "You sow much and bring in little" (Hag. 1:6), and now you say this to me? Which shall we believe, the first statement or the second?"

10. A. Zechariah went to give comfort. He said to the city, "The Holy One, blessed be He, has sent me to you to bring you comfort."
- C. She said to him, "What do you have in hand."
- D. He said to her, "I am very angry with the nations that are at ease" (Zech. 1:15).
- E. She said to him, "Yesterday, you said to me,' The Lord was very angry with your fathers' (Zech. 1:2), and now you say this to me? Which shall we believe, the first statement or the second?"

11. A. Malachi went to give comfort. He said to the city, "The Holy One, blessed be He, has sent me to you to bring you comfort."
- C. She said to him, "What do you have in hand."

D. He said to her, "All the nations shall call you happy, for you shall be a happy land" (Mal. 3:12).

E. She said to him, "Yesterday, you said to me, 'I have no pleasure in you says the Lord of hosts' (Mal. 1:10), and now you say this to me? Which shall we believe, the first statement or the second?"

12. A. The prophets went to the Holy One, blessed be He, saying to him, "Lord of the ages, Jerusalem has not accepted the comfort [that we brought her]."

B. Said to them the Holy One, blessed be He, "You and I together shall go and comfort her."

C. Thus we say: "Comfort, comfort my people" but read the letters for "my people" as with me.

D. Let the creatures of the upper world comfort her, let the creatures of the lower world comfort her.

E. Let the living comfort her, let the dead comfort her.

F. Comfort her in this world, comfort her in the world to come.

G. Comfort her on account of the Ten Tribes, comfort her on account of the tribe of Judah and Benjamin.

H. [Thus we must understand the statement, "Comfort, comfort my people, says your God. Speak tenderly to the heart of Jerusalem and cry to her that her warfare is ended, that her iniquity is pardoned, that she has received from the Lord's hand double for all her sins" (Is. 40:1-2) in this way:"] Comfort, comfort my people" but read the letters for my people as "with me. "

God's messages to Amos contained contradictions, as was the case with the other prophets.

Pesiqta deRab Kahana XVI:X

1. A. "[Comfort, comfort my people,] will your God say. [Speak tenderly to the heart of Jerusalem and cry to her that her warfare is ended, that her iniquity is pardoned, that she has received from the Lord's hand double for all her sins]" (Is. 40:1-2):

B. R. Hanina bar Pappa and R. Simeon:

C. [Focusing on the future tense of the phrase, Comfort, comfort my people, will your God say,] R. Hanina bar Papa said, "The Israelites said to Isaiah, 'Our lord, Isaiah, is it possible that you have come to comfort only that generation in the days of which the house of the sanctuary was destroyed?'

D. "He said to them, 'It is to all generations that I have come to bring comfort. What is said is not, Your God has said, but rather, Your God will say.'"

E. Said R. Simon, "The Israelites said to Isaiah, "Our lord, Isaiah, is it possible that all these things that you say you have made up on your own?'

4. Amos in Genesis Rabbah, Leviticus Rabbah, and Pesiqta deRab Kahana

F. "He said to them, 'It is to all generations that I have come to bring comfort. What is said is not, Your God has said, but rather, Your God will say.'"

G. Said R. Hinenah son of R. Abba, "In eight passages [Is. 1:11, 18, 33:10, 40:1, 25, 41:21 (twice), 66:9], it is written, Your God will say, matching the eight prophets who prophesied after the house of the sanctuary [was first destroyed] and these are they: Joel, Amos, Zephaniah, Haggai, Zechariah, Malachi, Ezekiel, and Jeremiah."

Amos is on a list of prophets of the indicated category.

Pesiqta deRab Kahana XIX:II

1. A. "Hear me when I groan, with no one to comfort me. [All my enemies, when they heard of my calamity, rejoiced at what you had done, but hasten the day you have promised when they shall become like me]" (Lam. 2:21):

2. A. Rabbis interpreted the cited verse to speak of the nations of the world:

   B. "You find that when the sins of Israel made it possible for the gentiles to enter Jerusalem, they made the decree that in every place to which they would flee, they should close [the gates before them].

   C. "They tried to flee to the south, but they did not let them: 'Thus says the Lord, for three transgressions of Gaza, yes for four, I will not reverse it [because they permitted an entire captivity to be carried away captive by delivering them up to Edom]' (Amos 1:6).

   D. "They wanted to flee to the east, but they did not let them: 'Thus says the Lord, for three transgressions of Damascus, yes for four, I will not reverse it' (Amos 1:3).

   E. "They wanted to flee to the north, but they did not let them: 'Thus says the Lord, for three transgressions of Tyre, yes for four, I will not reverse it' (Amos 1:21).

   F. "They wanted to flee to the west, but they did not let them: 'The burden upon Arabia' (Is. 21:13).

   G. "Said to them the Holy One, blessed be He, 'Lo, you outraged them.'

   H. "They said before Him, 'Lord of the ages, are you not the one who did it? [All my enemies, when they heard of my calamity, rejoiced at what you had done].'"

Israel was isolated from her neighbors at the time of her distress. Amos supplies proof of that fact.

Pesiqta deRab Kahana XX:II

3. A. Said R. Abba bar Kahana, "[With reference to the verse, 'The Lord make you...like Rachel and like Leah' (Ruth 4:11), the blessing

said by the guests at Boaz's wedding to Ruth], most of those assembled were of the side of Leah but they mentioned the name of Rachel first, as you say, 'And Rachel was barren' (Gen. 29:31)."

B. Said R. Isaac, "[Reading the letters of the word barren to sound the word the principal,] it is because Rachel was the principal of the household, as you say, 'And Rachel was barren' (Gen. 29:31)."

C. It was taught on Tannaite authority in the name of R. Simeon b. Yohai, "It is because everything depended on Rachel, therefore all of the children were called in her name: 'Rachel is weeping for her children' (Jer. 31:14).

D. "And it is not the end of the matter that they are called in her name, but even in the name of her son: 'Perhaps the Lord of hosts will show favor to the remnant of Joseph' (Amos 5:15).

E. "And even in the name of the son of her son: 'Is not Ephraim my favorite son' (Jer. 31:19). [All of these verses intend to speak of the whole of Israel.]"

Rachel was given the principal role in Israelite genealogy.

Pesiqta deRab Kahana XXIV:I

1. A. "Is a shofar blown in a city and the people are not afraid? Does evil befall a city [unless the Lord has done it?]" (Amos 3:6):

   B. The matter may be compared to the case of a town besieged by marauders, in which there was an elder who would warn all the people of the town [about the danger].

   C. Whoever listened to him was saved, and whoever did not listen was overcome by the guerillas, who killed him.

   D. So it is written: "So you, son of man, I have made a watchman for the house of Israel; [whenever you hear a word from my mouth, you shall give them warning from me]" (Ez. 33:7).

   E. "If I say to the wicked, O wicked man, you shall surely die, [and you do not speak to warn the wicked to turn from his way, that wicked man shall die in his iniquity, but his blood I will require at your hand. But if you warn the wicked to turn from his way and he does not turn from his way, he shall die in his iniquity, but you will have saved your life]" (Ez. 33:8).

   F. So too: Is a shofar blown in a city on the New Year,

   G. ...and the people are not afraid: this refers to Israel.

   H. Does evil befall a city unless the Lord has done it? (Amos 3:6):

   I. The Holy One, blessed be He, does not want the death of the wicked, in line with the following verse:

   J. "As I live, says the Lord God, I have no desire for the death of the wicked. [I would rather that a wicked man should mend his ways and live. Give up your evil ways, give them up, O Israelites, why should you die?]" (Ez. 33:11).

   K. [In Aramaic:] "O people, what do I want from you, but Give up your evil ways, give them up, O Israelites.

4. Amos in Genesis Rabbah, Leviticus Rabbah, and Pesiqta deRab Kahana

> L. There are those who prefer to derive the same lesson from the following: Seek me and live (Amos 5:4).
> M. [In Aramaic]: "O people, what do I want of you, but: Seek me and live."
> N. Therefore Hosea admonishes Israel, saying to them," Return O Israel to the Lord your God, [for you have stumbled because of your iniquity. Take with you words and return to the Lord and say to him, Take away all iniquity; accept that which is good, and we will render the fruit of our lips. Assyria shall not save us, we will not ride upon horses; and we will say no more, Our God to the work of our hands. In you the orphan finds mercy]" (Hosea 14:1-3).

Amos contributes the proposition that God brings punishment on those that deserve it, but prefers to forgive the repentant.

Pesiqta deRab Kahana XXVI:VII

> 1. A. It was taught in the name of R. Eliezer: "Nadab and Abihu died only because they gave instruction in the presence of Moses, their master."
> B. There was the case of a disciple who gave instruction in the presence of his master, R. Eliezer. He said to Imma Shalom, his wife, "He is not going to live out the week." The Sabbath had not come before he died.
> C. His students came and said to him, "Rabbi, are you then a prophet?"
> D. He said to them, "'I am not a prophet nor the disciple of a prophet' (Amos 7:14), but this is the tradition which I have received: 'Any (disciple) who teaches a law in his master's presence is liable to the death penalty.'"

Amos's denial of prophecy is cited in context.

5

Amos in Esther Rabbah I, Ruth Rabbah, Song of Songs Rabbah, Lamentations Rabbah and Abot deRabbi Natan

ESTHER RABBAH I

Esther Rabbah I III:i

1. A. R. Judah b. R. Simon opened by citing the following verse: "'as if a man fled from a lion and a bear met him; or went into the house and leaned with his hand against the wall, and a serpent bit him' (Amos 5:19)."

2. A. R. Huna and R. Aha in the name of R. Hama bar Hanina: "'as if a man fled from a lion:' this refers to Babylonia, called a lion: 'the first was like a lion' (Dan. 7:4).
   B. "'and a bear met him:' this speaks of Media, called a bear: 'And behold, another beast, a second, like a bear' (Dan. 7:5)."

3. A. R. Yohanan said, "The word for a bear is written defectively."
   B. That is consistent with the position of R. Yohanan, which is as follows: "'Therefore a lion out of the forest slays them' (Jer. 5:6): this speaks of Media.
   C. "'A leopard watches over their cities:' this is Greece.
   D "'Everyone who goes out of there is torn into pieces:' this is Edom."

4. A. [Reverting to 2.B:] "' or went into the house:'
   B. "This speaks of Greece in the time of the temple.
   C. "'and leaned with his hand against the wall, and a serpent bit him:' this speaks of Edom: 'The sound thereof shall go like the serpent's (Jer. 46:22)."

8. A. Another interpretation of the verse, "as if a man fled from a lion and a bear met him; or went into the house and leaned with his hand against the wall, and a serpent bit him" (Amos 5:19).
   B. "as if a man fled from a lion:" this speaks of Nebuchadnezzar.
   C. "and a bear met him:" this is Belshazzar.

D. "or went into the house and leaned with his hand against the wall, and a serpent bit him:" this is Haman, who hissed at people like a snake, as it is written, "Rehum the commander and Shimshai the scribe" — the latter is a son of Haman — "wrote a letter to Artaxerxes, the king, in this manner" (Ezra 4:8).

The sequence of beasts — lion/bear/serpent — is linked to Israel's history with Babylonia, Media, Greece, and then not Rome but Persia/Haman. That is accounted for, obviously, by the context, but it is an odd development.

Esther Rabbah I XI:i

5. A. And what is the greatness of that throne, "Moreover the king [Solomon] made a great throne of ivory" (2 Chr. 9:17)?
   B. Said R. Aha, "Is it not written, 'Now Ahab had seventy sons in Samaria' (2 Kings 10:1)."
   C. And said R. Hoshia the Elder, "As he had seventy sons in Samaria, so he had seventy in Jezreel."
   D. [Continuing B:] "And each had two palaces, one for winter, one for summer: 'And I will smite the winter house with the summer house' (Amos 3:15)."
   E. R. Judah b. R. Simon says, "Each had four: 'And the houses of ivory shall perish' (Amos 3:15)."
   F. Rabbis say, "Each had six: 'And the great houses shall have an end' (Amos 3:15)."
   G. And here merely: "Moreover the king [Solomon] made a great throne of ivory" (2 Chr. 9:17).

Amos's condemnation of the ostentatious self-indulgence of the wealthy is parsed in connection with the sons of Ahab.

Esther Rabbah I XXXII:i [=Leviticus Rabbah XII:I.1:]

13. A. Another interpretation of the verse, "In the end it bites like a snake and stings (PRS, also: separates) like an adder" (Prov. 23:32):
    B. Just as a viper distinguishes (PRS) between life and death, so wine caused a separation between the ten tribes in the matter of the exile.
    C. That is in line with what is written: "Woe to those who rise early in the morning, that they may run after strong drink, who tarry late in the evening till wine inflames them" (Is. 5:11).
    D. "Who drink wine in bowls" (Amos 6:6).
    E. On this account: "Therefore they shall now be the first of those who go into exile" (Amos 6:7).

As above.

Ruth Rabbah

Ruth Rabbah IV:i

3. A. [As to the verse, "Whose leaders are borne with. There is no breach and no going forth and no outcry" (Ps. 144:14)], R. Simeon b. Laqish would transpose the elements as follows:
   B. "When the elders bear with the youngsters, 'there is no breach' into exile: 'And you shall go out at the breaches' (Amos 4:3).
   C. "'...and no going forth': into exile: 'Cast them out of my sight and let them go forth' (Jer. 15:1).
   D. "'...and no outcry': of exile: 'Behold, the voice of the cry of the daughter of my people' (Jer. 8:19). 'And the cry of Jerusalem went up.'"
4. A. [As to the verse, "Whose leaders are borne with. There is no breach and no going forth and no outcry" (Ps. 144:14)], R. Luliani [Julius] said, "When the young listen to the old, but the old do not bear with the young, then 'The Lord will enter into judgment' (Is. 3:14).
   B. "'The name of the man was Elimelech': 'Because trouble has come, do you forsake them?'
   C. "'...and a certain man of Bethlehem in Judah went.'"

Amos provides a gloss on the word "breach" at Ps. 144:14.

Ruth Rabbah V:ii

1. A. "...there was a famine in the land, and a certain man of Bethlehem in Judah went to sojourn in the country of Moab, he and his wife and his two sons":
   B. [=Genesis Rabbah XXV:III.1:]Ten famines came into the world.
   C. One was in the time of Adam: "Cursed is the ground for your sake" (Gen. 3:17).
   D. One was in the time of Lamech: "Out of the ground which the Lord has cursed" (Gen. 5:29).
   E. One was in the time of Abraham: "And there was a famine in the land" (Gen. 12:10).
   F. One was in the time of Isaac: "And there was famine in the land, beside the first famine that was in the time of Abraham (Gen. 26:1).
   G. One was in the time of Jacob: "For these two years has the famine been in the land" (Gen. 45:6).
   H. One was in the time of the rule of judges: "And it came to pass in the days when the judges ruled, that there was a famine in the land" (Ruth 1:1).
   I. One was in the time of David: "There was a famine in David's time" (2 Sam. 21:1).
   J. One was in the time of Elijah: "As the Lord, the God of Israel, lives, before whom I stand, there shall not be dew or rain these years" (1 Kgs. 17:1).

K. One was in the time of Elisha: "And there was a great famine in Samaria" (2 Kgs. 6:25).
L. There is one famine which moves about the world.
M. One famine will be in the age to come: "Not a famine of bread nor a thirst for water but of hearing the words of the Lord" (Amos 8:11).

Amos prophesies an eschatological famine.

Ruth Rabbah IX:i

1. A. "...and both Mahlon and Chilion died":
   B. [Leviticus Rabbah XVII:IV.1-4:] R. Huniah in the name of R. Joshua b. R. Abin and R. Zechariah son-in-law of R. Levi in the name of R. Levi: "The merciful Lord does not do injury to human beings first. [First he exacts a penalty from property, aiming at the sinner's repentance.]
   C. From whom do you derive that lesson? From the case of Job: 'The oxen were plowing and the asses feeding beside them [and the Sadeans fell upon them and took them and slew the servants with the edge of the sword; and I alone have escaped to tell you' (Job 1:14). Afterward: 'Your sons and daughters were eating and drinking wine in their eldest brother's house, and behold, a great wind came across the wilderness and struck the four corners of the house, and it fell upon the young people, and they are dead' (Job 1:19).]"
   D. Now were the oxen plowing and the asses feeding beside them? Said R. Hama b. R. Hanina, "This teaches that the Holy One, blessed be He, showed him a paradigm of the world to come.
   E. "That is in line with the following verse of Scripture: 'The plowman shall overtake the reaper'" (Amos 9:13).

Amos prophesies the life of the world to come.

Ruth Rabbah LXXVIII:i

1. A. "Then all the people who were at the gate and the elders said, 'We are witnesses. May the Lord make the woman, who is coming into your house, like Rachel and Leah, who together built up the house of Israel. My you prosper in Ephrathah and be renowned in Bethlehem'":
   B. Said R. Berekhiah, "Most of the people present were of the line of Leah, therefore the statement treats Rachel as principal."
2. A. Said R. Abba b. Kahana, "Rachel was his principal wife:
   B. "'But Rachel was barren' (Gen. 29:31).
   C. "Do not read the letters as though they spelled 'barren,' but rather as though they spelled 'principal.'"

3. A. R. Simeon b. Yohai taught on Tannaite authority, "Because they spoke against Rachel [as barren], therefore all of Jacob's descendants are assigned to her:
B. "'Rachel is weeping for her children' (Jer. 31:15).
C. "Not only to her, but to her son: 'It may be that the Lord, God of hosts, will be gracious to the remnant of Joseph' (Amos 5:15).
D. "Not only to her son but to her grandson: 'Is Ephraim a darling son for me? is he not a child that is dandled?' (Jer. 31:20)."

Amos assigns Rachel's grandchildren to her.

Song of Songs Rabbah

Song of Songs Rabbah I:vii
1. A. "The Song of Songs":
B. the best of songs, the most excellent of songs, the finest of songs.
C. "Let us recite songs and praise the One who has made us a theme of song in the world: 'And they shall shout aloud the songs of the Temple' (Amos 8:3), that is, praise of the Temple."

Amos speaks of praise of the Temple.

Song of Songs Rabbah V:i
1. A. "I am very dark, but comely, [O daughters of Jerusalem, like the tents of Kedar, like the curtains of Solomon]" (Song 1:5):
B. "I am dark" in my deeds.
C. "But comely" in the deeds of my forebears.
2. A. "I am very dark, but comely":
B. Said the Community of Israel, "'I am dark' in my view, 'but comely' before my Creator."
C. For it is written, "Are you not as the children of the Ethiopians to Me, O children of Israel, says the Lord" (Amos 9:7):
D. "as the children of the Ethiopians" — in your sight.
E. But "to Me, O children of Israel, says the Lord."

"I am dark but comely" is read in light of Amos 9:7. God sees the Israelites as comely, even though they see themselves differently.

Song of Songs Rabbah VI:i
1. A. "Do not gaze at me because I am swarthy":
B. R. Simon commenced discourse by citing the following verse of Scripture: "'Do not slander a servant to his master' (Prov. 30:10).
C. "The Israelites are called servants: 'For to me the children of Israel are servants' (Lev. 25:55).
D. "The prophets are called servants: 'But he reveals his counsel to his servants the prophets' (Amos 3:7).

E. "Thus said the Community of Israel to the prophets, '"Do not gaze at me because I am swarthy."

F. "'None among my sons rejoiced more than Moses, but because he said, "Listen, please, you rebels" (Num. 20:10), he suffered the decree not to enter the land.'"

Israelites and prophets are referred to as God's servants, and one is not to slander a servant to his master, God.

Song of Songs Rabbah XXII:ii

6. A. R. Meir came forward and interpreted this verse: "'Now there dwelled an old prophet in Bethel' (1 Kgs. 13:11):

B. "And who was it? This was Amaziah, priest of Bethel [Amos 7:10]."

C. Said to him R. Yosé, "Meir, you're making scrambled eggs! Who was he really? He was Jonathan son of Gershom son of Moses: 'Jonathan, son of Gershom, son of Manasseh' (Judges 18:30).

Amos identifies the priest of Bethel.

Song of Songs Rabbah XXX:iv

9. A. Said R. Yohanan, [B. Sanhedrin 97A: Our Rabbis have taught on Tannaite authority]:

B. "The seven year cycle in which the son of David will come:

C. "As to the first one, the following verse of Scripture will be fulfilled: 'And I will cause it to rain upon one city and not upon another' (Amos 4:7).

D. "As to the second year, the arrows of famine will be sent forth.

E. "As to the third, there will be a great famine, in which men, women, and children will die, pious men and wonder-workers alike, and the Torah will be forgotten in Israel.

F. "As to the fourth year, there will be plenty which is no plenty.

G. "As to the fifth year, there will be great prosperity, and people will eat, drink, and rejoice, and the Torah will be restored to those that study it.

H. "As to the sixth year, there will be rumors.

I. "As to the seventh year, there will be wars.

J. "As to the end of the seventh year [the eighth year], the son of David will come."

K. Said Abbayye, "Lo, how many septennates have passed like that one, and yet he has not come."

Amos's prophesy that rain will fall selectively is given a place in the sequence of events of the seven years leading up to the advent of the Messiah.

Song of Songs Rabbah XXXII:i

1. A. "Catch us the foxes, the little foxes, [that spoil the vineyards, for our vineyards are in blossom]":

5. Amos in Esther Rabbah I, Ruth Rabbah, Song of Songs Rabbah...

B. When the other kingdoms are assigned metaphors, the metaphors pertain only to fire: "And I will set my face against them, out of the fire they have come fourth, and the fire shall devour them" (Ez. 15:7).

C. But when the Egyptians are assigned a metaphor, it is only that which is consumed by fire: "They are quenched as a wick" (Isa. 43:17).

D. When the other kingdoms are assigned metaphors, the metaphors pertain only to silver and gold: "As for that image, its head was of fine gold" (Dan. 2:32).

E. But when the Egyptians are assigned a metaphor, it is only lead: "They sank as lead" (Ex. 15:10).

F. When the other kingdoms are assigned metaphors, the metaphors pertain only to cedars: "Behold, the Assyrian was a cedar in Lebanon" (Ez. 31:3); "The tree that you saw, which grew" (Gen. 4:17); 'Yet I destroyed the Amorite before them, whose height was like that of cedars" (Amos 2:9).

G. But when the Egyptians are assigned a metaphor, it is only stubble: "It consumes them like stubble" (Ex. 15:7).

H. When the other kingdoms are assigned metaphors, the metaphors pertain only to beasts of pray: "And four great beasts came up from the sea, different from one another" (Dan. 7:3); "The first was like a lion" (Dan. 7:4).

I. But when the Egyptians are assigned a metaphor, it is only foxes: "Catch us the foxes, the little foxes."

Amos supplies a proof text to the proposition that the other kingdoms, besides Egypt, are assigned metaphors pertaining to cedars.

Song of Songs Rabbah XXII:ii

6. A. R. Meir came forward and interpreted this verse: "'Now there dwelled an old prophet in Bethel' (1 Kgs. 13:11):

B. "And who was it? This was Amaziah, priest of Bethel [Amos 7:10]."

C. Said to him R. Yosé, "Meir, you're making scrambled eggs! Who was he really? He was Jonathan son of Gershom son of Moses: 'Jonathan, son of Gershom, son of Manasseh' (Judges 18:30).

D. "Now the N in the name Manasseh is suspended, indicating that if he attained merit, he would be deemed the son of Moses, and if not, then he would be deemed the son of Manasseh [2 Kgs. 21]."

E. Associates asked before R. Samuel b. R. Nahman, saying to him, "How come a priest for an idol lived all those years?"

F. He said to them, "It was because he was stingy with the idol. [Simon: he tried to discourage idolatry.]

As above.

Song of Songs Rabbah LVIII:i

3. A. "For behold the Lord commands and the great house will be made into ruins and the small one into clefts" (Amos 6:11):
   B. "Ruins" are not the same as "clefts,"
   C. for a ruin yields fragments, and a cleft does not.

The word-choices of Amos are defined.

Song of Songs Rabbah LXXVI:i

1. A. "His speech is most sweet:"
   B. "For thus says the Lord to the house of Israel, seek me and live" (Amos 5:4).
   C. Do you have a candy sweeter to the palate than this?
   D. "As I live, says the Lord God, I have no pleasure in the death of the wicked" (Ezek. 33:11).
   E. Do you have a candy sweeter to the palate than this?
   F. "For I have no pleasure in the death of him who dies, says the Lord God, repent and live" (Ezek. 18:32).
   G. Do you have a candy sweeter to the palate than this?
   H. "When the wicked man turns away from his wickedness...and does what is lawful and right, he shall save his soul alive" (Ezek. 18:27).
   I. Do you have a candy sweeter to the palate than this?

God's message via Amos, "Seek me and live," exemplifies the sweetness of God's speech,

Song of Songs Rabbah CXI:iii

17. A. [Supply: "And this shall be peace: when the Assyrian shall come into our land, and when he shall tread in our palaces, then shall we raise against him seven shepherds:"]
    B. Who are the seven shepherds?
    C. David in the middle, to the right, Adam, Seth, and Methuselah; to the left, Abraham, Jacob, and Moses.
    D. Where is Isaac? He goes and takes a seat at the gate of Gehenna to deliver his descendants from the punishment of Gehenna.
    E. " and eight princes among men:"
    F. Who are the eight princes?
    G. Jesse, Saul, Samuel, Amos, Zephaniah, Hezekiah, Elijah, and the royal Messiah.

Amos is listed among the eight princes, not all of them prophets.

Lamentations Rabbah

Lamentations Rabbah II.ii.

1. A. "Thus says the Lord of hosts: 'Summon the dirge-singers, let them come; send for the skilled women, let them come.' [Let them quickly start a wailing for us, that our eyes may run with tears, our pupils flow with water. For the sound of wailing is heard from Zion, How are we despoiled! How greatly are we shamed!]" (Jer. 9:16-18).
   B. R. Yohanan and R. Simeon b. Laqish and rabbis [comment on the cited verse in different ways].
3. A. R. Simeon b. Laqish said, "The matter may be compared to the case of a king who had two sons. He lost his temper with the first, took a stick and beat him and the son writhed and perished.
   B. "He then lamented for him.
   C. He lost his temper with the second, took a stick and beat him and the son writhed and perished.
   D. "He said, 'Now I don't have the strength to lament for them, but summon the dirge-singers, let them come; send for the skilled women, let them come.'
   E. "So when the Ten Tribes went into exile, the Holy One, blessed be He, began to lament for them: 'Hear you this word that I take up in lamentation over you, O house of Israel' (Amos 5:1).
   F. "But when Judah and Benjamin went into exile, it is as though the Holy One, blessed be He, said, 'now I do not have the strength to lament for them, but "Summon the dirge-singers, let them come; send for the skilled women, let them come." Let them quickly start a wailing for us, [that our eyes may run with tears, our pupils flow with water].'
   G. "What is written is not 'for them' but 'for us,'
   H. "'it is for me and for them.'
   I. "'that our eyes may run with tears, our pupils flow with water:'
   J. "What is written is not, 'their eyes,' but 'our eyes,'
   K. "'mine and theirs.'"

God himself mourned for the Ten Tribes, so Amos, but he did not have the strength to mourn for Judah and Benjamin but summoned professional mourners for the purpose.

Lamentations Rabbah XXV.i.

3. A. In ten upward stages the Presence of God departed: from the cherub to the cherub, from the cherub to the threshold of the temple-building; from the threshold of the temple to the two cherubim; from the two cherubim to the eastern gate of the sanctuary; from the eastern gate of the sanctuary to the [wall of the] temple court; from the [wall of the] temple court to the altar; from the altar to the roof; from the roof to the city wall, from the city wall to the city, from the city to the Mount of Olives.

B. [From Pesiqta de Rab Kahana 13:11 supply: ...from the ark cover to the cherub: "And he rode upon a cherub and flew"(2 Sam. 22:11).]
C. ...from the cherub to the cherub: "And the glory of the Lord mounted up from the cherub to the threshold of the house" (Ezek. 10:45).
D. ...from the cherub to the threshold of the house: "And the glory of the God of Israel was gone up from the cherub, whereupon it was to the threshold of the house" (Ezek. 9:3).
E. ...from the threshold of the temple to the two cherubim: "And the glory of the Lord went forth from off the threshold of the house and stood over the cherubim" (Ezek. 10:18). Lo, it was necessary to say only, And the glory of the Lord came.... And you say, "went forth"? What is the meaning of "went forth"?
H. ...from the two cherubim to the eastern gate of the sanctuary: "The cherubs raised their wings and flew above the earth before my eyes" (Ezek. 10:9).
I. ...from the eastern gate of the sanctuary to the [wall of the] temple court: "And the courtyard was filled with the splendor of the glory of the Lord" (Ezek. 10:4).
J. ...from the [wall of the] temple court to the altar: "I saw the Lord standing beside the altar" (Amos 9:1).
K. ...from the altar to the roof: "It is better to dwell on the corner of the roof" (Prov. 21:9).
L. ...from the roof to the altar [Pesiqta: city wall]: "I saw the Lord standing beside the altar" (Amos 9:1).
M. ...from the altar to the wall: "and behold, the Lord was standing on the wall made by a plumb line " (Amos 7:7).
N. What is "a plumb line"?
O. It is the sanhedrin of seventy-one members.
P. How do we know?
Q. From the numerical value of the letters of the word for plumb line, which add up to seventy-one.
R. "And the Lord said, 'Behold, I will set a plumb line'" (Amos 7:8):
S. Said R. Judah bar Simon, "It was from the wall to the city, as it is said, 'Listen, the Lord cries to the city' (Micah 6:9)."
T. ...from the city to the Mount of Olives: "And the glory of the Lord went up from the midst of the city and stood on the

Amos supplies proof-texts for stages in the departure of God from the Temple.

Lamentations Rabbah XXXVI:iii.

7. A. "Is his mercy entirely gone forever? (Ps. 57:9):"
B. What is the meaning of the word translated "entirely"?
C. R. Reuben said, "It is a Greek word, aphes, meaning, let go: 'And he shall say, No, let go' (Amos 6:10)."

Amos gives a philological fact.

Lamentations Rabbah LV.i.
1. A. "Hear how I groan; there is none to comfort me. All my enemies have heard of my trouble:"
   F. Rabbis interpret the verse to speak of the destruction of Jerusalem.
   G. for when the Temple was destroyed, the nations of the world sent word everywhere to which the Israelites fled and shut them out.
   H. [Cohen, p. 145:] You find that every place where Israel attempted to flee, the inhabitants stopped them.
   I. They attempted to flee northwards but the people would not let them: "For three transgressions of Gaza, yes for four, I will not reverse it, because they carried away captive a whole captivity to deliver them up to Edom" (Amos 1:6).
   J. They tried to flee to the east but the people would not let them: "For three transgressions of Tyre, yes for four, I will not reverse it, because they delivered up a whole captivity to Edom and did not remember the covenant of brothers" (Amos 1:9).
   K. They attempted to flee to the west, but the people would not let them: "The burden upon Arabia. In the thickets of Arabia you shall lodge, O you caravans of Dedanites" (Isa. 21:13).

Amos provides proof that the neighboring frontiers of Israel were closed to the refugees.

Lamentations Rabbah LXXXVIII.i.
2. A. "let him put his mouth in the dust — there may yet be hope; let him give his cheek to the smiter and be filled with insults:"
   B. This is one of six verses of Scripture upon reaching which Rabbi [Judah the Patriarch] would weep.
   C. "And Samuel said to Saul, Why have you disturbed me, to bring me up" (1 Sam. 28:15).
   D. "For lo, he who forms the mountains and creates the wind and declares to a man what he is thinking" (Amos 4:13), thus implying that even minor actions are inscribed against someone on the record, and who inscribes them?
   E. "Who makes the morning darkness" (Amos 4:13).
   F. "Seek the Lord, all you humble of the earth" (Zeph. 2:3).
   G. "Hate evil and love good" (Amos 5:15). Why? "For God shall bring every work into judgment concerning every hidden thing, whether it be good or evil" (Qoh. 12:14).
   H. And this passage: "let him put his mouth in the dust — there may yet be hope; let him give his cheek to the smiter and be filled with insults."

Amos says that God sees even the innermost thoughts of man and records minor actions.

Abot deRabbi Natan

Abot deRabbi Natan VIII:III.
1 A. In the case of three disciples in session and occupied with study of the Torah, the Holy One, blessed be he, credits it to them as if they formed a single band before him,
 B. as it is said, "He who builds his upper chambers in the heaven and has founded his band upon the earth, he who calls for the waters of the sea and pours them out upon the face of the earth, the Lord is his name" (Amos 9:6).
 C. Thus you have learned that in the case of three disciples in session and occupied with study of the Torah, the Holy One, blessed be he, credits it to them as if they formed a single band before him.

The three disciples studying on their own are compared to water collected and poured out on the earth, "a single band" before God.

Abot deRabbi Natan IX:III.
5 A. At that time Aaron began to appease Moses. He said to him, My brother, Moses, have we ever done ill to anyone in the world?"
 B. He said to him, "No."
 C. He said to him, "Now if we have never done ill to anyone in the world, how should we do evil to you, our brother! But what can I do? It was a mistake on our side! We neglected the covenant between you and us, as it is said, 'And they did not remember the covenant of brothers' (Amos 1:9).
 D. "On account of the covenant that has been drawn up between us, which we have neglected, shall we now lose our sister?"
 E. At that moment Moses drew a little circle and stood in it and sought mercy for her, saying, "I am not going to move from here until you heal Miriam my sister," as it is said, "Let her not, I ask, be as a corpse" (Num. 12:12).
 F. At that moment the Holy One, blessed be he, said to Moses, "If a king had grown angry against her, if her father had grown angry with her, she would have had to bear the shame for seven days. I, the King of kings of kings, all the more so is it not proper that she should bear her shame for fourteen days? But on your account, it will be forgiven to her."
 G. So it is said, "And the Lord said to Moses, if her father should spit in her face" (Num. 12:14).

Amos provides a proof text for Aaron's proposition that he had forgotten the covenant between himself and his brother Moses.

Abot deRabbi Natan XXXIV:IX.

1 A. In ten upward stages the Presence of God departed, from one place to the next: from the ark cover to the cherub, from the cherub to the threshold of the temple-building; from the threshold of the temple to the two cherubim; from the two cherubim to the roof of the sanctuary; from the roof of the sanctuary to the wall of the temple court; from the wall of the temple court to the altar; from the altar to the city; from the city to the Temple mount; from the temple mount to the wilderness.

B. from the ark cover to the cherub: "And he rode upon a cherub and flew" (2 Sam. 22:11).

C. from the cherub to the threshold of the temple-building: "And the glory of the Lord mounted up from the cherub to the threshold of the house" (Ez. 10:45).

D. from the threshold of the temple to the two cherubim: "And the glory of the Lord went forth from off the threshold of the house and stood over the cherubim" (Ez. 10:18).

E. from the two cherubim to the roof of the sanctuary: "It is better to dwell in a corner of the housetop" (Prov. 21:9).

F. from the roof of the sanctuary to the wall of the temple court: "And behold the Lord stood beside a wall made by a plumbline" (Amos 7:7).

G. from the wall of the temple court to the altar: "I saw the Lord standing beside the altar" (Amos 9:1).

H. from the altar to the city: "Hark, the Lord cries to the city" (Mic. 6:9).

I. from the city to the Temple mount: "And the glory of the Lord went up from the midst of the city and stood upon the mountain" (Ez. 11:23).

J. from the temple mount to the wilderness: "It is better to dwell in a desert land" (Prov. 21:19).

K. And then to on high: "I will go and return to my place" (Hos. 5:15).

Amos contributes a stage to the upward journey of God's presence.

6

Amos in the Bavli

I. BERAKHOT

M. Ber. 1:1 III.

4 A. [Referring to Ps. 145], said R. Yohanan, "On what account is there no verse beginning with an N in Psalm 145?

B. "It is because the N starts the verse referring to the fall of (the enemies of) Israel.

C. "For it is written, 'Fallen (NPLH), no more to rise, is the virgin of Israel' (Amos 5:2)."

D. *In the West [the Land of Israel] the verse at hand is laid out in this way:* "Fallen, and no more to fall, the virgin of Israel will arise."

E. *Said R. Nahman bar Isaac, "Even so, David went and by the Holy Spirit brought together the N with the following letter of the alphabet, S: 'The Lord upholds (SMK) all those who fall (NPL) (Ps. 145:14)."*

Amos 5:2 is subjected to a close reading in the context of Ps. 145.

M. Ber. 2:8 I.

1 A. *What is the basis for Rabban Gamaliel's action [described at M. 2:6A]?*

B. *He took the view that the rules of mourning by night derive solely from the authority of rabbis [and that mourning rites apply only by day, so far as the requirement of the Torah is concerned].*

C. For it is written, "[And I will make it as the mourning for an only son] and the end thereof as a bitter day" (Amos 8:10). [Thus it is only by day that the bitterness of mourning applies].

D. *In a case in which one is frail, rabbis made no such decree [on which account Gamaliel felt free not to mourn by night, so he washed up].*

Amos confirms that on the authority of the Torah's law mourning takes place only by day, not by night.

M. Ber. 7:4-5 III.

12 A. Said R. Assi, "People are not to chatter over the cup for the blessing [at the Grace after Meals]."
B. And R. Assi said, "People do not say a blessing over a cup of punishment."
C. *What is a "cup of punishment"?*
D. Said R. Nahman bar Isaac, "The second cup of wine [since two is an unlucky number]."
E. *It has been taught on Tannaite authority along these same lines:*
F. He who drinks in pairs [an even number of cups of wine] should not say the blessing [Grace].
G. For it says, "Prepare to meet your God, Israel" (Amos 4:12). But this one is not prepared."

Preparation for meeting God in the recitation of the Grace after Meals involves not drinking an even number of cups of wine.

M. Ber. 8:5 VI.

1 A. The House of Shammai say, "Who created..." [M. 8:5C].
B. *Raba said, "Concerning the word 'bara' [created] everyone agrees that 'bara' implies [the past tense]. They differ concerning 'boré' [creates]. The House of Shammai reckon that 'boré' means, 'Who will create in the future. 'And the House of Hillel reckon that 'boré' also means what was created [in the past]."*
C. R. Joseph objected, "'Who forms light and creates darkness' (Isaiah 45:7), 'Creates mountains and forms the wind' (Amos 4:13) 'Who creates the heavens and spreads them out'" (Isaiah 42:5).
D. "But," R. Joseph said, "Concerning 'bara' and 'boré' everyone agrees that [the words] refer to the past. They differ as to whether one should say 'light' or 'lights.'"

Amos supplies a proof-text for the stated proposition.

M. Ber. 9:1-5 I.30

A. Said R. Joshua b. Levi, "He who in a dream sees a river, when he gets up should say, 'Behold I will extend peace to her like a river' (Is. 66:12). [This he should do] lest some other verse should come to mind before that one, such as, 'For distress will come in like a river' (Is. 59:19).
H. "He who in a dream sees a lion, when he gets up should say, 'The lion has roared, who will not fear' (Amos 3:8), lest another verse should come to mind first, such as, 'A lion is gone up from his thicket' (Jer. 4:7)."

The lion here represents God in Amos's prophesy.

M. Ber. 9:1-5 III.

2 A. Samuel contrasted these verses: "It is written, 'Who makes the Bear, Orion, and the Pleiades' (Job 9:9).
  B. "And elsewhere it is written, 'Who makes Pleiades and Orion' (Amos 5:8) [thus in different order].
  C. "How so? If it were not for the heat of Orion the world could not stand the cold caused by Pleiades, and if it were not for the cold of Pleiades, the world could not stand the heat caused by Orion.

Amos follows a different order from Job, yielding the stated message.

2 SHABBAT

M, Shab. 1:2 V.

7 A. *Said Abbayye, "As to our colleagues in Babylonia, from the perspective of him who has said, 'the recitation of the Evening Prayer is optional,' once they have loosened their belt, we don't bother them again [to stop the meal prior to saying the prayer]; from the perspective of him who has said that it is obligatory, do we trouble them to do so? Lo, the recitation of the Afternoon Prayer in the opinion of all parties is obligatory, and yet we have learned,* But if they began, they do not break off [what they were doing], **in connection with which said R. Hanina, 'That is after he has loosened his belt.'"**
  B. [10A] *At that time, drunkenness is uncommon, but here, at the evening meal, it is common [so one must refrain from the meal, even if he has loosened his belt, until prayers are said, if these prayers are deemed obligatory]. Or also, in the case of the afternoon prayer, since a set time is assigned to it, one will be concerned and not come to transgress; but as to the evening prayer, since no set time is assigned to it but it can be recited all night long, he will not be preoccupied about it and may end up transgressing.*
  C. *Objected R. Sheshet, "So is it such a big deal to loosen one's belt? Anyhow, let him get up as is and say the prayer?"*
  D. It is on the count of, "Prepare to meet your God, O Israel" (Amos 4:12).

V.8 A. *Rabbah bar R. Huna put on stockings and said his prayer, citing the verse,* **"Prepare to meet your God, O Israel" (Amos 4:12).**
  B. *Raba took off his cloak, clasped his hands, and said his prayer, saying, "I am like a slave before his master."*
  C. *Said R. Ashi, "I saw R. Kahana, when there was anguish in the world, removing his cloak, clasping his hands, and saying his prayers, with the words, 'I am like a slave before his master.' But*

when there was tranquillity in the world, he would put on and wrap himself in his cloak and pray, saying the verse, 'Prepare to meet your God, O Israel' (Amos 4:12)."

Amos provides the authority for the law governing conduct at prayer, here in connection with a meal.

M. Shab. 2:6 II.
> 4 A. **For the sin of robbery, locusts come up and famine follows, and people eat the flesh of their sons and daughters: "Hear this word, you cows of Bashan, who are in the mountain of Samaria, who oppress the poor, who crush the needy" (Amos 4:1).**
> B. *Said Raba, "For instance, the women of Mahoza, [33A] who eat but don't work."*
> C. And it is written, "I have smitten you with blasting and mildew; the multitude of your gardens and your vineyards and your figs trees and your olive trees has the palmer-worm devoured" (Amos 4:9); and further, "That which the palmer-worm has left has the locust eaten; that which the locust has left the cankerworm has eaten; that which the cankerworm has left the caterpillar has eaten" (Joel 1:4); "And one shall snatch on the right hand and be hungry and he shall eat on the left hand and they shall not be satisfied; they shall eat every man the flesh of his own arm" (Isa. 9:19). Don't read the consonants that yield "the flesh of his own arm" in that way but as though they bore vowels to yield "the flesh of his own seed."

Amos accounts for the natural disasters that are caused by immoral conduct, identifying the idol rich with the loss of crops.

M. Shab. 6:2 IV.
> 7 A. **"That lie on beds of ivory and stretch themselves on their couches" (Amos 6:9):**
> B. Said R. Yosé bar Hanina, "This teaches that they would who piss naked in front of their beds."
> C. But R. Abbahu ridiculed that statement: "If so, then notice what is written, 'Therefore shall they now go captive with the first that go captive' (Amos 6:7) — they who piss in front of their beds naked will go captive with the first who go captive! [That's disproportionate!]"
> D. "Rather," said R. Abbahu, "What it refers to is men who eat and drink with one another and push their beds together and trade wives with one another, and so 'they pollute their beds' with semen that doesn't belong to them."

Amos's indictment is spelled out.

6. Amos in the Bavli

M. Shab. 6:3 IV.
- 6 A. "And anoint themselves with the chief ointments" (Amos 6:6):
- B. Said R. Judah said Samuel, "This refers to spikenard oil."
- C. **Objected R. Joseph,** "Also against spikenard oil, too, did R. Judah b. Baba make a decree, but sages did not concur with him [T. Sot. 15:9H]. *Now, if you say it is on account of mere pleasure, then how come sages didn't agree with him?"*
- D. Said to him Abbayye, "Well, from your perspective, as to the statement, 'that drink in bowls of wine' (Amos 6:6) — R. Ammi and R. Assi — one said, 'It means a cup with spouts, from which several can drink at once; the other said, it means that they threw their goblets to one another — isn't that forbidden, too? But didn't Rabbah b. R. Huna visit the household of the exilarch, who drank from such a thing, and yet he didn't say a word to him?! Rather, whatever gives both pleasure and occasion for rejoicing did rabbis prohibit, but what is a luxury but not doesn't give occasion for rejoicing, they didn't prohibit."

Amos's language is amplified.

3 ERUBIN

I find no references to Amos.

4 PESAHIM

M. Pesahim I.1 3:7-8
- 5. A. Said R. Isaac, "Whoever derives benefit from an optional banquet in the end will go into exile: 'And you that eat lambs out of the flock and calves out of the midst of the stall' 'therefore now shall they go captive at the head of those who go captive' (Amos 6:4, 7)."

Amos's prophesy of punishment is clarified.

M. Pesahim 8:1 I:
- 11. A. Said R. Yohanan, "On what basis did Jeroboam son of Joash, king of Israel, have the unearned grace of being counted with the kings of Judah? Because he didn't accept gossip against Amos.
- B. "How do we know that he was counted with them? 'The word of the Lord that came to Hosea son of Beeri in the days of Uzziah, Jotham Ahaz, and Hezekiah, kings of Judah' (Hos. 1:1).
- C. "And how do we know that he didn't accept gossip? 'Then Amaziah priest of Beth el sent to Jeroboam king of Israel, saying, Amos has conspired against you' (Amos 7:10); 'for thus Amos said, 'Jeroboam shall die by the sword' (Amos 7:11). Said Jeroboam, 'God forbid,

that that righteous man could have said any such thing! But if he did say it, what can I do to him, since the Presence of God said it to him.'"

Jeroboam accepted the legitimacy of Amos's prophecy against him himself.

5 YOMA

M. Yoma 1:1 IV.
1 A. [The Counselor's Chamber:] *Our rabbis have taught on Tannaite authority:*
   B. All the chambers that were located in the sanctuary had no mezuzah except for the counselor's chamber, for in that chamber was the dwelling place of the high priest.
   C. Said R. Judah, "Now is it not the fact that there were any number of chambers in the sanctuary in which there were residences, and they had no mezuzah.
   D. "Rather, the operative consideration for the counselor's chamber's not having a mezuzah was a decree."
   E. *What is the operative consideration behind the opinion of R. Judah?*
   F. *Said Rabbah, "R. Judah takes the view that* any dwelling that is not made for use both in the dry season and in the rainy season is not classified as a house [that would require a mezuzah]." [Here we are talking about a temporary residence.]
   G. *Objected Abbayye, "But is it not written, 'And I will smite the winter house with the summer house' (Amos 3:15)?"*
   H. He said to him, "Both the winter house and the summer house are *classified as houses by name, but that is not so with the generic, 'house.'"*

Amos refers to temporary houses, whether generic or otherwise.

M. Yoma 8:8-9 III.
16. A. *It has been taught on Tannaite authority:*
    B. R. Yosé b. R. Judah says, "When a person does a transgression once, he is forgiven, a second time, he is forgiven, a third time, he is forgiven. But when he does it a fourth time, he is not forgiven: 'Thus says the Lord, for three transgressions of Israel, yes for four, I will not reverse it' (Amos 2:6); and further, 'Lo, all these things does God work, twice, yes, three times, with a man' (Job 33:29)."
    C. *What's the point of and further,?*
    D. *Should you say, that is the case when the public is involved, but not in the case of an individual [the cited verse proves the contrary, which speaks of an individual, not all Israel].then come and take note:* "Lo, all these things does God work, twice, yes, three times, with a man" (Job 33:29).

Amos places limits on the capacity of forgiveness manifested by God. He forgives thee transgressions, but not the fourth.

6 SUKKAH

M. Suk. 2:4B-D I.

3. A. Said R. Abba bar Zabeda said Rab, "A mourner is liable to carry out all of the religious duties that are stated in the Torah except for the religious duty involved in putting on the phylacteries.
   B. "For lo, in their regard, the word 'beauty' is stated."
   C. *[How so?] Since the All-Merciful said to Ezekiel, "Bind your beauty on you" (Ez. 24:17), [his sense is that] "You are the one who is obligated, but everyone else [who is in mourning] is exempt. [Ezekiel, in particular, is admonished to give up the normal rites of mourning. So he is told to put on his phylacteries. Other mourners are exempt from doing so.]*
   D. *That rule pertains to the first day [of mourning], since it is written,* "And the end thereof as a bitter day" (Amos 8:10). [Slotki, p. 109, n. 20: The beginning of the verse is, "And I will make it as the mourning for an only son." Since "day" in the singular is used, it follows that actual mourning is limited to one day.]

Amos's statement concerning mourning yields evidence on the law of mourning.

M. Suk. 5:1D-5:4 II.

17. A. "And this shall be peace: when the Assyrian shall come into our land, and when he shall tread in our palaces, then shall we raise up against him seven shepherds and eight princes among men" (Mic. 5:4).
    B. Who are the seven shepherds?
    C. David in the middle, Adam, Seth and Methuselah on his right, Abraham, Jacob and Moses, on his left.
    D. And who are the eight princes among men?
    E. Jesse, Saul, Samuel, Amos, Zephaniah, Zedekiah, the Messiah, and Elijah.

Amos is listed among the princes among men.

7 BESAH

I find nothing relevant.

8 ROSH HASHANAH

M. Rosh Hashanah 1:2E-H [I.9]

[A] *Our rabbis have taught on Tannaite authority:*

B. The former rain is called *yoreh* because it teaches [*moreh*] people to plaster their roofs, bring in their produce, and do all their needs [before the rainy season hits full-force].

C. Another matter: It is called *yoreh* [using the letters RWH] because it saturates the ground [RWH] and penetrates to the depths, as it is said, "Watering her ridges abundantly, settling down the furrows thereof, you make her soft with showers, you bless the growth thereof" (Ps. 65:11).

D. Another matter: It is called *yoreh* [using the letters RWH] because it descends gently and does not descend with fury.

E. Or perhaps it is called *yoreh* because it makes the fruit fall [referring to the word yoreh, to throw] and washes away seed and washes away trees?

F. To exclude that interpretation, the word "latter rain" [*malqosh*] is introduced: just as latter rain is for a blessing, so the former rain is only for a blessing.

G. But might the word for latter rain [*malqosh*, using the letters LQSH, Amos 7:1, grasshopper] bear the meaning, it knocks over houses and breaks trees and brings up crickets?

H. To exclude that interpretation, the word "former rain" is introduced: just as the former rain is only for a blessing, so the latter rain is only for a blessing.

I. *But how do we know that the former rain itself is only for a blessing?*

J. As it is written, "Be glad then you children of Zion and rejoice in the Lord your God, for he gives you the former rain in just measure and he brings down for you the rain, the former rain and the latter rain, as at the first" (Joel 2:21).

Amos provides a philological fact.

M. Rosh Hashanah 1:1-2D

M.. And said R. Hisda, "Rains that fell on part of the country but on part of the country did not fall are not classified in the category, 'And he will shut up.'"

N. *Is that so now? And has it not been written,* "And I also have withheld the rain from you when there were yet three months to the harvest, and I made it rain on one city and not on another, one piece was rained upon and not another" (Amos 4:7), in which connection said R. Judah said Rab, "Both of them represent a curse"!

6. Amos in the Bavli

O. *There is no contradiction here. In the one case Scripture speaks of rain that comes in excess, in the other, rain that comes as required."*

P. Said R. Ashi, "A careful reading of the matter yields that conclusion also, for the word 'it will rain' is used, made up of the three letters that stand for the words, let it be a place of rain, thus meaning, a place flooded by rain."

Q. *That proves the point.*

The interpretation of Amos 4:7 is subjected to a close reading. It is meant as a curse in all its elements.

9 TAANIT

M. Taanit 1:1-2D I.

14 [M] And said R. Hisda, "Rains that fell on part of the country but on part of the country did not fall are not classified in the category, 'And he will shut up.'"

N *Is that so now? And has it not been written,* "And I also have withheld the rain from you when there were yet three months to the harvest, and I made it rain on one city and not on another, one piece was rained upon and not another" (Amos 4:7), *in which connection said R. Judah said Rab, "Both of them represent a curse"!*

O *There is no contradiction here. In the one case Scripture speaks of rain that comes in excess, in the other, rain that comes as required."*

P Said R. Ashi, "A careful reading of the matter yields that conclusion also, for the word 'it will rain' is used, made up of the three letters that stand for the words, let it be a place of rain, thus meaning, a place flooded by rain."

Q *That proves the point.*

As above.

10 MEGILLAH

I find no reference to Amos.

11 MOED QATAN

M. Moed Qatan 3:1-2 II.

15. A. A mourner is forbidden to do work, since it is written, "And I shall turn your feasts into mourning" (Amos 8:10) — just as on a festival it is forbidden to do work, so a mourner is forbidden to do work.

B. What is the rule as to an excommunicated person's doing work?

C. Said R. Joseph, *"Come and take note:* When sages said that it is forbidden for those who are fasting to do work, they said that this was the case only in daytime, but at night it is permitted, and the same applies also to one who has been excommunicated and to a mourner. *Does this not, then, refer to all restrictions?"*

D. *Not, it refers to other items on the list but not to doing work.*
E. *Come and take note:* As to a person who is excommunicated, he may repeat Mishnah-teachings, and others may repeat Mishnah-teachings to him, he may be hired and others may be hired by him.
F. *That proves the matter.*
G. What about a person afflicted with the skin ailment?
H. *The question stands.*

Amos implies that there is an analogy between mourning and the Festival, with the result that the rules of the Festival apply to the day of mourning.

M. M.Q. 3:3 II.1.

A. But was Kush the name of that Benjaminite? Wasn't it Saul? But just as a Kushite [Ethiopian] has a skin that is different, so Saul did deeds that were distinguished.
B. Along these same lines you may explain the following:
C. "And Miriam and Aaron spoke against Moses because of the Kushite woman that he had married" (Num. 12:1):
D. Now was she [called] Kushite? Was her name not Zipporah? But just as a Kushite [Ethiopian] has a skin that is different, so Zipporah did deeds that were distinguished.
E. Along these same lines you may explain the following:
F. "Now Ebed Melekh the Kushite heard" (Jer. 38:7):
G. Now was he [called] Kushite? Was his name not Zedekiah? But just as a Kushite [Ethiopian] has a skin that is different, so Zedekiah did deeds that were distinguished.
H. Along these same lines you may explain the following:
I. "Are you not like the children of Kushites to me, O Children of Israel, says the Lord" (Amos 9:7):
J. But is their name Kushites? Are they not Israelites?
K. But just as a Kushite [Ethiopian] has a skin that is different, so the Israelites are distinguished by their deeds from all other nations.

Amos's meaning is inferred from the prevailing proposition.

M. M.Q 3:5-6 I.

12. A. *In session R. Hiyya bar Abba and R. Ammi and R. Isaac Nappaha under the awning of R. Isaac b. Eleazar. This matter came up among them:* "How do we know on the basis of Scripture that mourning is for a period of seven days? As it is written, 'And I shall turn your feasts into mourning, and I will make it as the mourning for an only son' (Amos 8:10) — just as the Feast [that is, Tabernacles] is for seven days, so the mourning is for seven days."

B. *Well, why not invoke the analogy of Pentecost [which is one day]?*
C. *That analogy is required for the matter explained by R. Simeon b. Laqish, for said R. Simeon b. Laqish in the name of R. Judah the Patriarch, "How on the basis of Scripture do we know that mourning on account of news of a bereavement that has come from a great distance applies only for a single day? As it is written, 'And I shall turn your feasts into mourning, and I will make it as the mourning for an only son' (Amos 8:10) — just as the Pentecost is a feast that lasts one day [so here too the mourning is for only one day]."*

Amos's meaning is inferred from the prevailing proposition.

M. M.Q. 3:5-6 I.

22. A. *Our rabbis have taught on Tannaite authority:*
    B. "A mourner is forbidden to put on his prayer boxes containing verses of Scripture for the first three days of his bereavement. From the third and onward, and the third is included, it is permitted for him to put them on. And if new people came to pay their respects, he does not remove them," the words of R. Eliezer.
    C. R. Joshua says, "A mourner is forbidden to put on his prayer boxes containing verses of Scripture for the first two days of his bereavement. From the second and onward, and the second is included, it is permitted for him to put them on. And if new people came to pay their respects, he does remove them."
    D. *Said R. Mattenah, "What is the scriptural basis for the position of R. Eliezer? It is written, 'And the days of weeping in the mourning for Moses were ended' (Dt. 34:8) [There are three key words, days, weeping, mourning, hence three days]."*
    E. *Said R. Ina, "What is the scriptural basis for the position of R. Joshua? It is written, 'And I will turn your feasts into mourning...and I will make it as the mourning for an only son and the end therefore as a bitter day' (Amos 8:10) [so the essential period of mourning is one bitter day]."*
    F. *And does not R. Joshua have to take account of the verse, "And the days of weeping in the mourning for Moses were ended" (Dt. 34:8)?*
    G. *He will say to you, "Moses was exceptional, because the mourning for him was enormous."*

As above.

12 HAGIGAH

M. Hag. 1:1-2 VI:

10. A. When R. Assi came to this verse, he wept: "Hate the evil and love the good and establish justice in the gate, perhaps the Lord, the

God of hosts, will be gracious" (Amos 5:15). *He said, "After all that, merely 'perhaps'?!"*

Amos portrays a bleak moral situation.

M. Hag. 1:1-2 VI.28.

A. *R. Ila was once walking up the stairs of Rabbah bar Shila. He heard a child's voice, reciting this verse:* "For lo, he who forms the mountains and creates the wind and declares to man what his conversation was" (Amos 4:13). He said, "A slave whose master tells him what his conversation was — has he any remedy?"

Amos prophesies that God knows man's innermost thoughts.

M. Hag. 1:3-5 VIII.1 3.

A. *Said Abbayye, "The House of Shammai, R. Eleazar, and R. Ishmael all take the view that* the burnt offering that the Israelites offered in the wilderness was the appearance offering. *The House of Hillel, R. Aqiba, and R. Yosé the Galilean, all take the view that* the burnt offering that the Israelites offered in the wilderness was the daily whole offering."
B. The House of Shammai: as we have just said.
C. *R. Ishmael: as has been taught on Tannaite authority:*
D. R. Ishmael says, "The generative principles were set forth at Sinai, [6B] but the details were set forth only in the tent of meeting." [Freedman: hence until the tent of meeting was set up, burnt offerings were not flayed and cut up.]
E. R. Aqiba says, "The generative principles and also the details were set forth at Sinai; they were repeated in the tent of meeting; they were restated yet again in the plains of Moab."
F. *Now if you take the view that* the burnt offering that the Israelites offered in the wilderness was the daily whole offering, *then is there the possibility that at first the sacrifice did not require flaying and chopping up but only later on would require flaying and chopping up?*
G. *R. Eleazar: as has been taught on Tannaite authority:*
H. It is a daily whole offering, which was offered at Mount Sinai" (Num. 28:6):
I. R. Eleazar says, "While the rites concerning it were stated at Sinai, the offering itself was not presented." [Abraham: so the burnt offerings brought by the young men of Ex. 24:5 must have been appearance offerings.]
J. R. Aqiba says, "It was offered up and was never discontinued."
K. Then how am I to interpret the verse, "Did you bring me sacrifices and offerings in the wilderness for forty years, O House of Israel" (Amos 5:25) [which suggests that regular public offerings were not offered]?

L. The tribe of Levi, which did not serve the idol, were the ones who offered it up.

Amos is understood to declare that while the Israelites did not present offerings in the wilderness, the Levites did.

M. Hag. 1:8 III.1

A. festal offerings...have little Scripture for many laws:
B. *But these are stated in writing in Scripture itself [at Ex. 12:14, Lev. 23:41]!*
C. *No, the observation is required in line with what R. Pappa said to Abbayye, "How do we know that the verse, 'and you shall keep it a feast to the Lord' (Lev. 23:41) means that one makes a sacrifice? Maybe the sense of the Torah is, 'celebrate a festival'?"*
D. *If so, then when Scripture says,* "That they may hold a feast to me in the wilderness" (Ex. 5:1) — *does that also mean merely, "celebrate a festival"? And should you say, yes indeed! isn't it written,* "And Moses said, You must also give into our hand beasts for killing and burnt offerings" (Ex. 10:25)?
E. *But maybe this is the sense of Scripture:* "Eat and drink and celebrate a festival before me"?
F. *Don't imagine it! For it is written,* "Neither shall the fat of my feast remain all night until the morning" (Ex. 23:18) — *so if you think that all this means is, celebrate a festival, then is there fat associated with a festival?*
G. *But maybe this is the sense of the All-Merciful:* Neither shall the fat that is offered during the course of my feast remain all night until the morning?
H. *Well, then, that would bear the sense, only during the festival may fat not remain overnight, but through the ordinary days of the year, it may remain overnight, but by contrast:* "All night unto morning" (Lev. 6:2) [which speaks of the entire year, not only festivals]!
I. *But maybe if I had to derive the fact from that verse alone, I would know it only as a positive commandment, and Scripture presented the other verse as a negative one?*
J. *There already is a negative commandment, in the verse:* "Neither shall any of the meat which you sacrifice the first day at evening remain all night until the morning" (Ex. 12:14).
K. *But maybe that is required to impose liability for violating two negative commandments and a positive one?*
L. *Rather, the appearance of the word "wilderness" which occurs in two distinct passages yields the point, namely: here we find,* "that they may hold a feast for me in the wilderness" (Ex. 5:5) *and elsewhere,* "Did you bring to me sacrifices and offerings in the wilderness" (Amos 5:25). *Just as the latter verse refers to sacrifices, so the former does.*

The Israelites, Amos proves, did present sacrifices in the wilderness.

M. Hag. 2:1 III.1
    A. **the works of creation [Gen. 1-3] before two:**
9. A. *Our rabbis have taught on Tannaite authority:*
    B. The House of Shammai say, "Heaven was created first, then the earth was created: 'In the beginning God created heaven and earth' (Gen. 1:1).
    C. And the House of Hillel say, "The earth was created first, then heaven: 'In the day that the Lord God made earth and heaven' (Gen. 2:4)."
    D. Said the House of Hillel to the House of Shammai, "In accord with your view, someone first builds the upper story, and then the basic house itself: 'It is he who builds his upper chambers in the heaven and has founded his vault upon the earth' (Amos 9:6)."
    E. Said the House of Shammai to the House of Hillel, "In your view a person makes the footstool first, then the throne: 'Thus says the Lord, the heaven is my throne and the earth is my footstool' (Is. 66:1)."
    F. But sages say, "Both were created at the same instant: 'Yes, my hand has laid the foundation of the earth, and my right hand has spread out the heavens; when I call to them they stand up together' (Is. 48:13)."

Amos contributes to the debate on cosmogony.

M. Hag. 2:1 III 16.
    A. *It has been taught on Tannaite authority:*
    B. R. Yosé says, "Woe for people who see but don't know what they're seeing, stand but don't know what they're standing on.
    C. "As to the earth, on what does it stand? On pillars: 'Who sakes the earth out of her place and the pillars thereof tremble' (Job 9:6).
    D. "As to the pillars, they stand on water: 'To him who spread forth the earth above the waters' (Ps. 136:6).
    E. "As to the waters, they are on the mountains: 'The waters stood above the mountains' (Ps. 104:6).
    F. "The mountains are on the wind: 'For lo, he who forms the mountains and creates the wind' (Amos 4:13).
    G. "The wind is on the storm: 'The wind, the storm makes its substance' (Ps. 148:8).
    H. "And the storm is suspended from the arm of the Holy One, blessed be he: 'And underneath are the everlasting arms' (Dt. 33:27)."
    I. But sages say, "The world rests on twelve pillars: 'He set the borders to the peoples according to the number of the tribes of the children of Israel' (Dt. 32:8)."
    J. And others say, "Seven pillars: 'She has hewn out her seven pillars' (Prov. 9:1)."

K. R. Eleazar b. Shammua says, "On one pillar, called righteous: 'But righteous is the foundation of the world' (Prov. 10:25)."

Amos holds that the mountains are formed on the foundation of the wind.

13 YEBAMOT

I find nothing relevant.

14 KETUBOT

M. Ket. 6:6 I.15
- A. Said R. Abbahu, "How on the basis of Scripture do we know that the mourner reclines at the head at the mourner's meal? 'I chose out their way and sat chief and dwelt as a king in the army, as one comforts the mourners' (Job 29:25)."
- B. "As one comforts the mourners" – *does that not mean that he was head of comforting others?*
- C. *Said R. Nahman bar Isaac, "Since the word is written with consonants that can be read* 'as when one comforts mourners,' [this conclusion may follow]."
- D. Mar Zutra said, "Proof derives from this verse: 'And the prince be he who is embittered, distraught among those stretched on couches' (Amos 6:7)" [following the rendition of Lazarus].

Amos supplies a proof-text for the stated proposition.

M. Ket. 13:11 III.10
- A. Ulla would regularly go up to the Land of Israel. He died abroad. They came and told R. Eleazar. He said, "You, Ulla – 'should you die in an unclean field' (Amos 7:17)?"
- B. They told him, "His bier has come."
- C. He said to them, "Being gathered in [to the Land] when alive is not the same thing as being gathered into the Land after death."

Amos refers to dying outside of the Holy Land, which alone is free of cultic contamination.

15 NEDARIM

M. Nedarim 4:3A-E III.8
- A. Said R. Yohanan, "All of the prophets were wealthy.
- B. "How do we know it? From the cases of Moses, Samuel, Amos, and Jonah.
- C. "Moses: 'I have not taken one ass from them' (Num. 16:15) – *now if he meant, without paying a fee for its use, then is all that he*

         claimed merely that he wasn't one of those who take without paying a fee? So what he must have meant was, even paying a fee [he had no need to hire animals because he had enough of his own]!"

D.   But maybe he was too poor to pay a fee for renting an animal?

E.   Rather, proof derives from "'hew for yourself two tablets of stone like the first' (Ex. 34:1) – the chips will belong to you.

F.   "Samuel: 'Behold, here I am: bear witness against me before the Lord and before his anointed: whose ox have I taken, or whose ass have I taken' (1 Sam. 12:3) – *now if he meant, without paying a fee for its use, then is all that he claimed merely that he wasn't one of those who take without paying a fee? So what he must have meant was, even paying a fee [he had no need to hire animals because he had enough of his own]!"*

G.   But maybe he was too poor to pay a fee for renting an animal?

H.   Rather, proof derives from "And his return was to Ramah, for there was his house" (1 Sam. 7:17), on which said Raba, "Wherever he went, his entire retinue went with him."

I.   Said Raba, "What is said of Samuel is greater than what is said of Moses. In the case of Moses: 'I have not taken one ass from them' – even for a fee; in the case of Samuel, he did not do so even with their knowledge and consent, 'And they said, you have not defrauded us nor taken advantage of our willingness' (1 Sam. 12:4)."

J.   "Amos: 'Then answered Amos and said to Amaziah, I was no prophet nor was I a disciple of a prophet, but I was a herdsman and harvester of sycamore fruit' (Amos 7:14)." *This was translated by R. Joseph, "Behold, I am the owner of flocks and of sycamore trees in the valley."*

K.   "Jonah: 'And he found a ship going to Tarshish, so he paid the fare thereof and went down into it' (Jonah 1:3)." And in this connection noted R. Yohanan, "He paid for the rent of the whole ship."

L.   R. Romanos said, "The fee to rent the whole ship was four thousand gold denarii."

The proof that Amos was a wealthy man lies in the rendition of his statement that he was a herdsman and harvester of sycamore trees to mean, he owned herds and orchards.

16 NAZIR

I find nothing.

17 SOTAH

M. Sot. 1:9 III.1

A.   And so it is on the good side: Miriam, etc. [M. 1:9A]:

6. Amos in the Bavli

M. Sot. 1:9 III.2.
- A. "And his sister stood afar off" (Ex. 2:4):
- B. Said R. Isaac, "This entire version of Scripture is stated with reference to the Presence of God:
- C. "'And stood,' as it is written, 'The Lord came and stood' (1 Sam. 3:10).
- D. "'His sister,' as it is written, 'Say to wisdom, you are my sister' (Prov. 7:4).
- E. "'Afar off,' as it is written, 'The Lord appeared from afar to me' (Jer. 31:3).
- F. "'To know,' as it is written, 'For the Lord is a God of knowledge' (1 Sam. 2:3).
- G. "'What,' as it is written, 'What does the Lord require of you' (Deut. 10:12).
- H. "'Done,' as it is written, 'Surely the Lord God will do nothing' (Amos 3:7).
- I. "'To him,' as it is written, 'And called it [him] Lord is peace' (Jud. 6:24)."

Amos provides a text in the clarification of how God was present with Miriam when she hid baby-Moses in the Nile.

M. Sot. 3:4D IV.1
- A. But if nothing happened, if she had merit, she would, etc. [M. 3:4D]:
- B. *In accord with the position of what authority is the Mishnah-paragraph [M. 3:4E] at hand?*
- C. *It does not accord with Abba Yosé b. Hanan, Eliezer b. Isaac of Kefar Derom, R. Ishmael.*
- D. *For we have learned on Tannaite authority:*
- E. "If the woman had merit [and the water did not affect her], one may attribute [the good fortune] to that source for a period of three months, the period it takes to recognize that she is pregnant [by the other man]," the words of Abba Yosé b. Hanan.
- F. R. Eliezer b. Isaac of Kefar Darom says, "Nine months, as it is said, 'Then she shall be free and shall conceive a child' (Num. 5:27), and elsewhere it is written, 'A seed shall serve him, it shall be related' (Ps. 22:31) — a seed that is worthy of being related."
- G. R. Ishmael says, "Twelve months. And even though there is no clear proof for that proposition, there is at least suggestive support for it, in the following verse of Scripture: 'Therefore O King, let my counsel be acceptable to you and break off your sins by righteousness, and your iniquities by showing mercy to the poor [21A], if there may be a lengthening of your tranquility' (Dan. 4:24), and it is further written, 'All this came upon King Nebuchadnezzar' (Dan. 4:25), and it is further written, 'At the end of twelve months' (Dan. 4:26)."

H. *The passage [M. 3:4E] indeed accords with the view of R. Ishmael, and he found a verse of Scripture, which he cited and then repeated.*
I. For it is written, "Thus says the Lord, 'For three transgressions of Edom' (Amos 1:11). [Cohen, p. 105, n. 11: "The respite of a year is trebled and this period corresponds to that given in the Mishnah."]
J. *What is the meaning of,* "Although there is no clear proof for that proposition..."? [Surely there is adequate proof.]
K. *But the case of gentiles [of whom Amos speaks, so too Daniel] may be different, for [God] does not visit judgment on them [right away, but only at the end of days].*

Amos's proof is as explained by Cohen's note.

M. Sot. 7:5 X.1

A. Blessings and curses — how so? When Israel came across the Jordan, etc. [M. 7:5A-B]:
30. A. *A Tannaite statement:*
B. A hornet did not cross [the Jordan] with them.
C. Indeed not? And is it not written, "And I shall send the hornet before you" (Ex. 23:28)?
D. Said R. Simeon b. Laqish, "It stood on the other side of the Jordan and squirted poison which blinded [the Canaanites'] eyes on top and castrated them on the bottom.
E. "For it is written, 'Yet I destroyed the Amorite before them, whose height was like the height of the cedars, and he was strong as the oaks, yet I destroyed his fruit from above and his roots from beneath' (Amos 2:9)."
F. *R. Papa said, "There were two hornets, one for Moses, the other for Joshua. The one for Moses did not cross the river, the one for Joshua did."*

God's provision for the Israelites to conquer the Amorites forms part of the amplification of the narrative of crossing the Jordan.

18 GITTIN

I find nothing in Bavli Gittin.

19 QIDDUSHIN

M. Qid. 4:1 V.26

A. **Ulla visited in Pumbedita the household of R. Judah. Seeing that R. Isaac b. R. Judah was mature but not yet married, he said to him, "How come the master hasn't married off his son to a wife?"**
B. *He said to him, "So do I know where to get one of correct genealogy?"*

6. Amos in the Bavli

C. *He said to him, "So do we know whence we descend? Maybe we come from those of whom it is written, 'They raped women in Zion, the virgins in the cities of Judah' (Lam. 5:11). And should you reply, if a gentile or a slave has sexual relations with an Israelite woman, the offspring is valid, so then maybe we come from those of whom it is written, 'that lie on beds of ivory and pollute themselves on their couches' (Amos 6:4). And said R. Yosé bar Hanina, 'This refers to men who piss naked in front of their beds,' but R. Abbahu ridiculed that statement: 'If so, then notice what is written, "Therefore shall they now go captive with the first that go captive" (Amos 6:7) – they who piss in front of their beds naked will go captive with the first who go captive! [That's disproportionate!]' Rather, said R. Abbahu, 'What it refers to is men who eat and drink with one another and push their beds together and trade wives with one another, and so "they pollute their beds" with semen that doesn't belong to them.'" [The upshot is that their children are mamzerim, and that is indelible.]*
D. *He said to him, "So what should I do?"*
E. *He said, "Look for the irenic ones [avoiding contentious families, for contention marks genealogical unfitness]."*
F. *For the Western families [the ones in the Land of Israel] make a test. When two are fighting, they observe which one falls silent first. They conclude, "This one is of superior genealogy."*

The clarification of Amos's statement has a bearing on the Halakhic pedigree of families.

20 Baba Qamma

I find no reference to Amos.

21 Baba Mesia

M. Baba Mesia 4:10 I.11.
A. Said R. Hisda, "All gates are locked, except for the gates that receive complaints against overreaching, as it is said, 'Behold, the Lord stood by a wall of wrongs, and in his hand were the wrongs' (Amos 7:7)."
B. Said R. Eleazar, "Penalty for all matters is exacted through an agent [angel], except for the penalty for overreaching, as it is said, 'And in his hand were the wrongs' (Amos 7:7)."

Amos holds that God penalizes those that overreach and wrong their fellows.

22 BABA BATRA

M. Baba Batra 1:6 IV.6
    A. Our rabbis have taught on Tannaite authority:
    B. This is the correct order of the prophets: Joshua, Judges, Samuel, Kings, Jeremiah, Ezekiel, Isaiah, the twelve prophets.

IV.7 A. *Let's consider:*
    B. *Hosea came first:* "God spoke first to Hosea" (Hos. 1:2).
    C. But did he speak first of all with Hosea? And were there not any number of prophets from Moses to Hosea?
    D. And said R. Yohanan, "He was the first of the group of four prophets who prophesied at that time: Hosea, Isaiah, Amos, and Micah."
    E. *So should not Hosea come first?*
    F. *Well, since his prophesies are written down along with those of Haggai, Zechariah, and Malachi, and since Haggai, Zechariah, and Malachi are designated as the conclusion of prophecy, he is reckoned along with them.*
    G. *So why not write out his prophecy on its own and put it first?*
    H. *Well, his scroll is so small that if copied on its own it might get lost.*

IV.8 A. *Let's consider:*
    B. *Isaiah in point of fact is prior to Jeremiah and Ezekiel, so why should he not be located first in line?*
    C. *Since the end of the book of Kings is about the destruction, and Jeremiah is wholly devoted to destruction, and Ezekiel starts off with destruction but ends up with consolation, while Isaiah is wholly consolation, we locate destruction adjacent to destruction, consolation to consolation.*

IV.9 A. **This is the correct order of the writings: Ruth, Psalms, Job, Proverbs, Qohelet, Song of Songs, Lamentations, Daniel, the scroll of Esther, Ezra, and Chronicles.**

IV.10 A. *From the perspective of him who says that* **Job lived in the time of Moses,** *should not Job come up at the first?*
    B. *We are not going to commence with a record of suffering.*
    C. *Yeah, well, Ruth is also about suffering.*
    D. *But that is about suffering with a happy ending, in line with what R. Yohanan said, for* said R. Yohanan, "Why was she called Ruth? Because from her came forth David, who lavished on the Holy One, blessed be He, hymns and praises."

Amos is included among the contemporaries, Isaiah, Hosea, and Micah.

M. Baba Batra 2:3E-J I.17
    A. R. Dimi from Nehardea brought a load of figs in a boat. Said the exilarch to Raba, "Go, see, if he is a neophyte rabbi, then assign him a market."

6. Amos in the Bavli

    B.   Raba said to R. Ada bar Abba, "Go, smell his jar [of wine, that is, test his learning]."
    C.   *He went and asked him, "If an elephant swallowed a twig basket and expelled it with his shit, what is the law [as to whether or not it is still a utensil, therefore subject to uncleanness, or is it simply shit]?"*
    D.   *He didn't know.*
    E.   *He said to R. Adda, "Are you Raba?"*
    F.   *He tapped his sandal and said to him, "Between me and Raba is there a considerable distance! Nonetheless, I can be your master, and Raba, the master of your master."*
    G.   *So they did not assign a market to him, and his figs were a total loss.*
    H.   *He came before R. Joseph and said to him, "Look, master, at what they did to me!" He said to him, "He who did not hold back vengeance for the wrong done to the king of Edom will not hold back the vengeance for the wrong done to you, as it is written, 'Thus says the Lord, for three transgressions of Moab, yes for four, I will not turn away the punishment thereof, because he burned the bones of the king of Edom into lime'* (Amos 2:1).
    I.   *So R. Adda bar Abba died.*

God exacted punishment for the wrong done to the King of Edom, so Amos.

M. Baba Batra 5:1A-D IV.3

    A.   Said Raba, "The rowboat and the lighter are pretty much the same thing. But R. Nathan, who was a Babylonian, uses the word familiar to him, as people use that word in Babylonia when referring to the rowboat that is used at the shallows, and Sumkhos, who was from the Land of Israel, used the word that is familiar to him, as people say in the verse, 'And your residue shall be taken away in lighters' (Amos 4:2)."

Amos's word choice registers.

M. Baba Batra 5:9 III.18

    A.   Our rabbis have taught on Tannaite authority:
    B.   Concerning those who store up produce, lend money on usury, falsify measures, and price-gouge, Scripture says, "Saying, when will the new moon be gone, that we may sell grain, and the Sabbath, that we may set forth grain? Making the ephah small and the sheqel great and falsifying the balances of deceit" (Amos 8:5). And in their regard, Scripture states, "The Lord has sworn by the pride of Jacob, surely I will never forget any of their works" (Amos 8:7).
    C.   *What would be an example of those who store up produce?*

D. Said R. Yohanan, "Like Shabbetai the produce hoarder."

The detail of the cited verse of Amos is clarified.

23 SANHEDRIN

M. Sanhedrin 1:1-6 II.22

A. There was a man who went around saying, "Happy is the one who hears [something] and remains indifferent. A hundred evils pass him by."
B. Said Samuel to R. Judah, "A verse of Scripture is written along these same lines: 'He who lets out water [of strife] causes the beginning of judgment' (Prov. 17:14). [The numerical value of the Hebrew letters for the word for judgment is a hundred], thus, it is the beginning of a hundred evils."
C. There was a man who went around saying, "For two or three acts of theft, the criminal is not put to death [but he ultimately will be caught]."
D. Said Samuel to R. Judah, "There is a pertinent verse of Scripture: 'So says the Lord, For three transgressions of Judah but for four I will not reverse [the judgment]' (Amos 2:6)."

Amos maintains that justice is ultimately done, if not immediately.

M. Sanhedrin 4:5 V.15

A. The emperor said to Rabban Gamaliel, "He who created the mountains did not create the wind, as it is said, 'For lo, there is one who forms mountains and one who creates wind' (Amos 4:13)."
B. "But how about this verse having to do with Adam: 'And he created...' (Gen. 1:27) 'and he formed...' (Gen. 2:7)? Here too, will you claim that the one who created this did not create that one?
C. "There is an area of a handbreadth square in man, with two apertures [the eye and the ear], and since it is written, 'He who plants the ear, shall he not hear, he who forms the eye, shall he not see' (Ps. 94:9), here too, will you say that the one who created this did not create that?"
D. He said to him, "Yes."
E. He said to him, "When someone dies, the two [creators] have to be brought to a common opinion."

The emperor cites Amos to prove that there is more than one God who creates.

M. Sanhedrin 10:5B III.5

A. A Tannaite authority repeated before R. Hisda, "He who holds back his prophecy is flogged."

6. Amos in the Bavli

B. *He said to him, "He who eats dates out of a sieve is flogged! Who warned [the prophet who withheld his prophecy, since no one could have known about that fact]? [No admonition, no flogging!]"*
C. *Said Abbayye, "His fellow prophets."*
D. *"How did they know about it?"*
E. *Said Abbayye, "For it is written, 'Surely the Lord will do nothing unless he reveals his secret to his servants, the prophets, (Amos 3:7)."*
F. *"But perhaps [the heavenly messengers] retracted?"*
G. *"If it were the case that they had retracted, they would have informed all the other prophets."*
H. *"And lo, there is the case of Jonah, in which heaven had retracted [its decision], but they had not notified Jonah."*
I. *"To begin with, Jonah was told that Nineveh would be turned, but he was not informed whether it was for good or for bad."*

God reveals his secrets to the prophets, who are privy to his plans, so Amos.

M. Sanhedrin 11:1-2 I.81

A. *Said R. Nahman to R. Isaac, "Have you heard when the son of 'the fallen one' will come?"*
B. *He said to him, "Who is the son of 'the fallen one'?"*
C. *He said to him, "It is the Messiah."*
D. *"Do you call the Messiah 'the son of the fallen one'?"*
E. *He said to him, "Yes, for it is written, 'On that day I will raise up [97A] the tabernacle of David, the fallen one' (Amos 9:11)."*
F. *He said to him, "This is what R. Yohanan said, 'The generation to which the son of David will come will be one in which disciples of sages grow fewer,*
G. *"'and, as to the others, their eyes will wear out through suffering and sighing, and troubles will be many, and laws harsh, forever renewing themselves so that the new one will hasten onward before the old one has come to an end.'"*

Amos proves that the son of 'the fallen one' is the son of David, hence the messiah.

M. Sanhedrin 11:1-2 I.82

A. *Our rabbis have taught on Tannaite authority:*
B. *The seven year cycle in which the son of David will come:*
C. *As to the first one, the following verse of Scripture will be fulfilled: "And I will cause it to rain upon one city and not upon another" (Amos 4:7).*
D. *As to the second year, the arrows of famine will be sent forth.*

E. As to the third, there will be a great famine, in which men, women, and children will die, pious men and wonder-workers alike, and the Torah will be forgotten by those that study it.
F. As to the fourth year, there will be plenty which is no plenty.
G. As to the fifth year, there will be great prosperity, and people will eat, drink, and rejoice, and the Torah will be restored to those that study it.
H. As to the sixth year, there will be rumors.
I. As to the seventh year, there will be wars.
J. As to the end of the seventh year [the eighth year], the son of David will come.
K. Said R. Joseph, "Lo, how many *septennates have passed like that one, and yet he has not come."*
L. Said Abbayye, *"Were there rumors in the sixth year and wars in the seventh year? And furthermore, did they come in the right order?"*

Amos spoke of the septennate in which the Messiah would come when he spoke of rain falling here but not there.

M. Sanhedrin 11:1-2 I.106

A. *So said R. Yohanan, "Let him come, but let me not see him."*
B. *Said R. Simeon b. Laqish to him, "What is the scriptural basis for that view? Shall we say that it is because it is written,* 'As if a man fled from a lion and a bear met him, or went into the house and leaned his hand on the wall and a serpent bit him' (Amos 5:19)?
C. "Come and I shall show you an example of such a case in this world.
D. "When a man goes out to the field and bailiff meets him, it is like one whom a lion meets. He goes into town and a tax-collector meets him, it is like one whom a bear meets.
E. "He goes into his house and finds his sons and daughters suffering from hunger, it is like one whom a snake bit.
F. "Rather, it is because it is written, 'Ask you now and see whether a man travails with child? Why do I see every man with his hands on his loins, as women in travail, and all faces are turned into paleness' (Jer. 30:6)."

Amos spoke of the concrete case of a man who fled a lion only to meet up with a bear and so forth. Simeon b. Laqish gives illustrations drawn from family life and everyday transactions.

M. Sanhedrin 11:1-2 I.110

A. *R. Simlai interpreted the following verse: "What is the meaning of that which is written,* 'Woe to you who desire the day of the Lord! to what end is it for you? the day of the Lord is darkness and not light' (Amos 5:18)?

6. Amos in the Bavli

B. "The matter may be compared to the case of the cock and the bat who were waiting for light.
C. "The cock said to the bat, 'I am waiting for the light, for the light belongs to me, but what do you need light for [99A]?'"
D. *That is in line with what a min said to R. Abbahu, "When is the Messiah coming?"*
E. *He said to him, "When darkness covers those men."*
F. *He said to him, "You are cursing me."*
G. *He said to him, "I am merely citing a verse of Scripture:* 'For behold, the darkness shall cover the earth, and great darkness the people, but the Lord shall shine upon you, and his glory shall be seen upon you' (Is. 60:2)."

Amos's statement on the day of the Lord is given an exegesis.

24 MAKKOT

M. Mak. 3:15-16 II.1

A. **Therefore he gave them abundant Torah and numerous commandments:**
B. R. Simelai expounded, "Six hundred and thirteen commandments were given to Moses, three hundred and sixty-five negative ones, corresponding to the number of the days of the solar year, and two hundred forty-eight positive commandments, corresponding to the parts of man's body."
C. *Said R. Hamnuna, "What verse of Scripture indicates that fact?* 'Moses commanded us Torah, an inheritance of the congregation of Jacob' (Dt. 33:4). *The numerical value assigned to the letters of the word Torah is* **[24A]** *six hundred and eleven, not counting,* 'I am' *and* 'you shall have no other gods,' *since these have come to us from the mouth of the Almighty."*
D. [Simelai continues:] "David came and reduced them to eleven: 'A Psalm of David: Lord, who shall sojourn in thy tabernacle, and who shall dwell in thy holy mountain? (i) He who walks uprightly and (ii) works righteousness and (iii) speaks truth in his heart and (iv) has no slander on his tongue and (v) does no evil to his fellow and (vi) does not take up a reproach against his neighbor, (vii) in whose eyes a vile person is despised but (viii) honors those who fear the Lord. (ix) He swears to his own hurt and changes not. (x) He does not lend on interest. (xi) He does not take a bribe against the innocent' (Psalm 15)."
E. "He who walks uprightly:" this is Abraham: "Walk before me and be wholehearted" (Gen. 17:1).
F. "and works righteousness:" this is Abba Hilqiahu.
G. "speaks truth in his heart:" for instance R. Safra.
H. "has no slander on his tongue:" this is our father, Jacob: "My father might feel me and I shall seem to him as a deceiver" (Gen. 27:12).

I. "does no evil to his fellow:" he does not go into competition with his fellow craftsman.
J. "does not take up a reproach against his neighbor:" this is someone who befriends his relatives.
K. "in whose eyes a vile person is despised:" this is Hezekiah, king of Judah, who dragged his father's bones on a rope bed.
L. "honors those who fear the Lord:" this is Jehoshaphat, king of Judah, who, whenever he would see a disciple of a sage, would rise from his throne and embrace and kiss him and call him, "My father, my father, my lord, my lord, my master, my master."
M. "He swears to his own hurt and changes not:" this is R. Yohanan.
N. For said R. Yohanan, "I shall continue fasting until I get home."
O. "He does not lend on interest:" not even interest from a gentile.
P. "He does not take a bribe against the innocent:" such as R. Ishmael b. R. Yosé.
Q. "He who does these things shall never be moved:"
R. When Rabban Gamaliel *reached this verse of Scripture, he would weep, saying, "If someone did all of these [virtuous deeds], then he will never be moved, but not merely on account of one of them."*
S. They said to him, "Is it written, 'Who does all of these things;'? What is written is only 'who does these things,' meaning, even one of them."
T. "For if you do not say this, then there is another verse of Scripture of which we have to take account: 'Do not defile yourselves in all of these things' (Lev. 18:24). Does this mean that one is unclean only if he touches all of these things, but not if he touches only one of them? But does it not mean, only one of them:?
U. "Here too it means that only one of these things is sufficient."
V. [Simelai continues:] "Isaiah came and reduced them to six: '(i) He who walks righteously and (ii) speaks uprightly, (iii) he who despises the gain of oppressions, (iv) shakes his hand from holding bribes, (v) stops his ear from hearing of blood (vi) and shuts his eyes from looking upon evil, he shall dwell on high' (Isaiah 33:25-26)."
W. "He who walks righteously:" this is our father, Abraham: "For I have known him so that he may command his children and his household after him" (Gen. 18:19).
X. "speaks uprightly:" this is one who does not belittle his fellow in public.
Y. "he who despises the gain of oppressions:" for example, R. Ishmael b. Elisha.
Z. "shakes his hand from holding bribes:" for example, R. Ishmael b. R. Yosé.
AA. "stops his ear from hearing of blood:" *who will not listen to demeaning talk about a disciple of rabbis and remain silent.*
BB. *For instance, R. Eleazar b. R. Simeon.*

6. Amos in the Bavli

CC. "and shuts his eyes from looking upon evil:" that is in line with what R. Hiyya bar Abba said.

DD. For said R. Hiyya bar Abba, "This is someone who does not stare at women as they are standing and washing clothes.

EE. Concerning such a man it is written, "he shall dwell on high."

FF. [Simelai continues:] "Micah came and reduced them to three: 'It has been told you, man, what is good, and what the Lord demands from you, (i) only to do justly and (ii) to love mercy, and (iii) to walk humbly before God' (Micah 6:8)."

GG. "only to do justly:" this refers to justice.

HH. "to love mercy:" this refers to doing acts of loving kindness.

II. "to walk humbly before God:" this refers to accompanying a corpse to the grave and welcoming the bread.

JJ. And does this not yield a conclusion a fortiori: if matters that are not ordinarily done in private are referred to by the Torah as "walking humbly before God," all the more so matters that ordinarily are done in private.

KK. [Simelai continues:] "Isaiah again came and reduced them to two : 'Thus says the Lord, (i) Keep justice and (ii) do righteousness' (Isaiah 56:1).

LL. "Amos came and reduced them to a single one, as it is said, 'For thus says the Lord to the house of Israel. Seek Me and live.'"

MM. *Objected R. Nahman bar Isaac, "Maybe the sense is, 'seek me' through the whole of the Torah?"*

NN. Rather, [Simelai continues:] "Habakkuk further came and based them on one, as it is said, 'But the righteous shall live by his faith' (Habakkuk 2:4)."

Amos reduced the entire panoply of the commandments to a single one, which covers them all.

M. Mak. 3:15-16 II.2.

A. Said R. Yosé bar Hanina, "Four decrees did our lord, Moses, make against Israel. Four prophets came along and annulled them.

B. "Moses said, 'And Israel dwells in safety alone at the fountain of Jacob' (Dt. 33:28). Amos came and annulled it: 'Then I said, O Lord God, stop, I ask you, how shall Jacob stand alone, for he is small,' and it goes on, 'The Lord repented concerning this: This also shall not be, says the Lord god' (Amos 7:5-6).

C. "Moses said, 'And among those nations you shall have no repose' (Dt. 28:65). Jeremiah came and annulled it: 'Thus says the Lord, the people that were left of the sword have found grace in the wilderness, even Israel, when I go to provide him rest' (Jer. 31:1).

D. "Moses said, 'The Lord...visits the sin of the fathers upon the children and upon the children's children to the third and to the fourth generation' (Ex. 34:7), but Ezekiel said, 'the soul that sins it shall die' (Ez. 18:3-4).

E. "Moses said, 'And you shall perish among the nations' (Lev. 26:38), but Isaiah said, 'And it shall come to pass in that day that a great horn shall sound and they shall come who were lost in the land of Assyria' (Is. 27:13)."

Amos nullified the decree that Israel would stand alone.

25 Shabuot

I found no references to Amos

26 Abodah Zarah

M. Abodah Zarah 1:1 I.13
A. *R. Abbahu praised R. Safra to the* minim [in context: Christian authorities of Caesarea], *saying that he was* a highly accomplished authority. *They therefore remitted his taxes for thirteen years.*
B. *One day they came upon him and said to him, "It is written, 'You only have I known among all the families of the earth; therefore I will visit upon you all your iniquities' (Amos 3:2). If one is angry, does he vent it on someone he loves?"*
C. *He fell silent and said nothing at all. They wrapped a scarf around his neck and tortured him. R. Abbahu came along and found them. He said to them, "Why are you torturing him?"*
D. *They said to him, "Didn't you tell us that he is* a highly accomplished authority, *but he does not know how to explain this verse!"*
E. *He said to them, "True enough, I told you that he was a master of Tannaite statements, but did I say anything at all to you about his knowledge of Scripture?"*
F. *They said to him, "So how come you know?"*
G. *He said to them, "Since we, for our part, spend a lot of time with you, we have taken the task of studying it thoroughly, while others [in Babylonia, Safra's place of origin] do not study [Scripture] that carefully."*
H. *They said to him, "So tell us."*
I. He said to them, "I shall tell you a parable. To what is the matter comparable? To the case of a man who lent money to two people, one a friend, the other an enemy. From the friend he collects the money little by little, from the enemy he collects all at once."

Amos says that God will exact punishment from the Israelites for all their iniquities little by little.

27 HORAYOT

I found no references to Amos

28 ZEBAHIM

M. Zebahim 12:1 III.6

A. **What is the conflict of Tannaite statements to which reference has been made [by Hisda]? It is as has been taught on Tannaite authority:**
B. For how long a spell is one in the status of a bereaved person [forbidden to eat sacrificial meat] on his account? The whole day [but not the night following].
C. Rabbi says, "So long as the corpse has not yet been buried."
D. *Now what is at issue here? Shall we say that it is the day on which the death takes place? Then does anyone reject the position that it is on the authority of rabbis that the day of death encompasses the night following it? Moreover, the language is,* Rabbi says, "So long as the corpse has not yet been buried." *So if the corpse has been buried, the man is permitted to eat sacrificial meat. And is there anybody who rejects the sense of the language,* "and the end thereof as a bitter day" (Amos 8:10) [which shows that the prohibitions affecting the bereaved person last the whole day of death inclusive of the time after burial]?
E. *Said R. Sheshet, "At issue here is the day of burial."*
F. *Objected R. Joseph, "Then when it is taught,* The day on which one hears of the death of a close relative and the day on which the bones of one's parents are collected for secondary burial — in both instances, one immerses and eats the sacrificial meat in the evening — *therefore as to the day of burial, one may not eat sacrificial meat even in the evening, with whom shall that statement concur?* [Freedman: both Rabbi and rabbis here hold that the evening is permitted.] *Rather, this is how to lay out matters:* For how long a spell is one in the status of a bereaved person [forbidden to eat sacrificial meat] on his account? The whole day [but not the night following]. Rabbi says, 'So long as the corpse has not yet been buried, but if he has been buried, it is the day alone, not including the night that follows.'"
G. *When this matter was stated before R. Jeremiah, he said, "Should an eminent authority such as R. Joseph say something like this? Then shall we suppose that Rabbi took the more lenient position? Surely it has been taught on Tannaite authority:* 'For how long a spell is one in the status of a bereaved person [forbidden to eat sacrificial meat] on his account? So long as the corpse has not been buried, and even from now and for ten days,' the words of Rabbi. And sages say, 'The bereavement pertains only to that day alone.' *Rather, this is how to lay out the matter:* For how long a

spell is one in the status of a bereaved person [forbidden to eat sacrificial meat] on his account? The whole day [but not the night following]. Rabbi says, 'So long as the corpse has not yet been buried, but if he has been buried, the day of burial takes hold of the night that follows.'"

H. *When this matter was presented in the presence of Raba, [he said,] "Since Rabbi took the position that, on the authority of rabbis, the day of burial takes hold of the night that follows, it must also be inferred that on the authority of Scripture itself the day of death takes hold of the night that follows."*

I. *But does Rabbi really take the view that on the authority of Scripture [not only of rabbis,] the status of bereavement pertains to the night? And has it not been taught on Tannaite authority:*

J. "'...and the end thereof as a bitter day' (Amos 8:10) — by day I am forbidden, by night I am permitted [so the status of bereavement by night derives from Scripture], but, as for the generations to come thereafter, the prohibition applies both by day and by night [and the night following is marked by the status of bereavement, in accord with the authority of Scripture]," the words of R. Judah.

K. Rabbi says, "The bereavement by night is a status that derives not from the teachings of the Torah but from the teachings of scribes."

L. *In point of fact it derives from the teaching of rabbis [scribes],* [101A] *but sages reinforced their teachings by imposing a more stringent rule than the one that Scripture has laid down.*

Amos 8:10 serves its established purpose of allowing the inference of laws of mourning.

29 MENAHOT

M. Menahot 3:5 XI.1

A. the four [kinds] which are in the lulab [Lev. 23:40],

B. It is written, "You shall take" (Lev. 23:40) — one act of taking of them all.

C. Said R. Hanan bar Raba, "This [rule that all kinds must be in hand] has been stated only in a case in which one did not have all of them, but if he had them all, then one does not invalidate the other [if they are not bound together in a single handful]."

D. *To that proposition an objection was raised:* Among the four species that are joined in the *lulab*, two produce fruit, and two do not produce fruit. Those that produce fruit are to be joined to those that do not, and those that do not are to be joined to those that do. And one does not carry out the pertinent obligation concerning them unless all of them form a single bundle. And so it is in regard to Israel's pleasing God, that too takes place only when all of them form a single community, in line with this verse: "He who builds

6. *Amos in the Bavli* 111

      his chambers in heaven and has founded his community upon earth" (Amos 9:6).
- E. *What we have here is a conflict of Tannaite formulations, for it has been taught on Tannaite authority:*
- F. **The lulab, whether bound with others or not —**
- G. **R. Judah says, "If it is bound up, it is valid, and if it is not bound up, it is not valid" [T. Suk. 2:10A-B].**
- H. *What is the scriptural basis for the position of R. Judah?*
- I. *By means of a verbal correspondence he draws an analogy because the word "taking" occurs both in the present context and in the setting of the bunch of hyssop [used in the purification rites of the person afflicted with the skin ailment, Lev. 14:4]. Just as in that context, what is required is that a bundle be made, so here too, what is required is that a bundle be made.*
- J. *And rabbis?*
- K. *They draw no such analogy established by the common appearance of the same word, "taking."*
- L. *In accord with which of the two positions is the following, which has been taught on Tannaite authority:*
- M. The proper performance of the religious duty in regard to the lulab is to bind the species together, but if one has not done so, it is valid.
- N. *In accord with which party is that statement? Now this cannot be in accord with R. Judah, for if one has not bound the species together, why should the arrangement be valid?*
- O. *And it can hardly accord with rabbis [vis à vis Judah], for why should it be an element of the religious duty [to do so at all, if they say one need not do so]?*
- P. Indeed, the statement accords with rabbis, and what is the sense of "religious duty"? It is on the count of, "This is my God and I will glorify him" (Ex. 15:2), which means one should be glorified before him through carrying out religious duties [in an especially felicitous manner, but if one does not do things exactly in that way, the action remains valid].

Amos's statement that God has founded his community on earth indicates that Israel pleases God only when it is unified and forms a single community, not a collection of sects.

30 HULLIN

M. Hullin 3:6-7 I.4

- A. Said Caesar to R. Joshua b. Hananiah, "Your God is like a lion. As it is stated, 'The lion has roared; who will not fear? [The Lord God has spoken; who can but prophesy?]' (Amos 3:8)." *What is exceptional about this? Any horseman can kill a lion. He [Joshua] said to him, "He is not like any lion. He is like the lion of Be Ilai."*

B. *He said to him, "You must show it to me."*
C. *He [Joshua] said to him, "You cannot see it. [That lion is too terrifying.]"*
D. *He said to him, "Really! Show it to me!"*
E. *He [Joshua] prayed.*
F. *It was uprooted from its place [and started to be transported toward them]. When it was four hundred parasangs away it gave out a single roar. All of the pregnant women of Rome miscarried [from fright] and all the walls fell down [from the vibrations]. When it was three hundred parasangs away it gave out another roar. All of the teeth of the people [of Rome] fell out [of their mouths from the impact of the sound]. And he [Caesar] himself fell from his throne to the ground.*
G. *He said to him [Joshua], "I beg you. Pray that it go back to its place."*
H. *He prayed and it went back to its place.*

God is compared by Amos to a lion, but the comparison is disproportionate.

M. Hullin 3:5 I.6

A. *R. Simeon b. Pazzi raised a contradiction: It is written, "And God made the two great lights." And it is written, "The greater light [to rule the day], and the lesser light [to rule the night; he made the stars also]." (Gen. 1:16). Said the moon to the Holy One, blessed be He, "Master of the Universe. it is possible to have two kings serve with one crown?" He said to her, "Go and be smaller." She said to him, "Master of the Universe. [Is it fair that] because I said to you something that is proper, that I have to make myself smaller?" He said to her, "Go and rule over both the day and the night."*
B. *She said to him, "What is the purpose of this? What good is a lamp in the daylight?" He said to her, "Go so that Israel will be able to calculate through you the days and the years." She said to him, "It is not possible to calculate the seasons without the sun. For it is written, 'Let them be for signs and for season and for day and for years" (Gen. 1:14).*
C. *[He said to her,] "Go forth. And righteous men shall be called by your name." [The moon was named the "lesser light," i.e., the small light. Jacob the Patriarch, the Tannaite authority Samuel and King David were called "small."]* Jacob was called small ["When they had finished eating the grass of the land, I said, 'O Lord God, forgive, I beseech thee! How can Jacob stand? He is so small!'" (Amos 7:2)]. Samuel [the Tannaite authority was called] the small one. David was called small ["David was the youngest [i.e., smallest]; the three eldest followed Saul" (I Sam. 17:14)].
D. *He saw that she was not placated.* Said the Holy One, blessed be He, "May I attain atonement because I made the moon smaller."

6. Amos in the Bavli

E. *And about this said R. Simeon b. Laqish,* "What is different about the goat offering for the new moon. For it is said regarding it, '[Also one male goat for a sin offering] to the Lord; [it shall be offered besides the continual burnt offering and its drink offering]' (Num. 28:15). Said the Holy One, blessed be He, "May I attain atonement because I made the moon smaller."

Amos refers to Jacob as small.

M. Hul. 6:4 E-G I.1

F. *Come and take note:* A certain Sadducee said to Rabbi, "The one who formed the mountains did not create the winds. And the one who created the winds did not form the mountains. *For it is written,* 'For lo, he who forms the mountains, and creates the wind' (Amos 4:13)."

G. *He said to him, "Fool! Look at the end of the verse,* '[For lo, he who forms the mountains, and creates the wind, and declares to man what is his thought; who makes the morning darkness, and treads on the heights of the earth] — the Lord, the God of hosts, is his name!' (Amos 4:13)."

H. *He said to him, "Give me three days and I will return with a decisive refutation."*

I. *Rabbi sat and fasted for three days. When he was about to eat they said to him, "A Sadducee is at the gate."*

J. *He said,* "They gave me poison for food" (Ps. 69:21).

K. He said to him, "Rabbi, I bring you good tidings.

L. He [the other one] could not find an answer and he threw himself off the roof and died."

M. He said to him, "Do you wish to dine with me?"

N. He said to him, "Yes."

O. After they ate and drank he [Rabbi] said to him, "Would you prefer to drink the cup [of wine over which you will recite] the blessings? Or would you rather have forty gold coins?"

P. He said to him, "I would rather drink the cup over which one recites the blessings."

Q. A heavenly echo went forth and proclaimed, "The cup of wine over which one recites the blessings is worth forty gold coins."

R. Said R. Isaac, "They still consider that family [of the opponent of Rabbi] among the greatest in Rome. And they call it the family of Bar Lulianus."

Here the *min*, called a Sadducee, reads Amos to refer to two creators, one for the mountains, one for the wind. But the same verse refers to a single actor who forms mountains and creates the wind.

31 Bekhorot

M. Bekhorot 7:6T-X IV.1

A. the giant:
B. R. Zebid taught on Tannaite authority, "That means someone very tall."
C. *Is this so? And has not R. Abbahu taught on Tannaite authority,* "How do we know that the Holy One, blessed be he, finds glory in tall people? 'Yet I destroyed the Amorite before them, who was as tall as the cedars' (Amos 2:9)."
D. Said R. Pappa, "'The giant' here is one who was tall, thin, and unshapely."

The quality of height is not a blemish, so Amos.

32 Arakhin

M. Arakhin 3:5 XI.1

A. the four [kinds] which are in the lulab [Lev. 23:40],
B. It is written, "You shall take" (Lev. 23:40) — one act of taking of them all.
C. Said R. Hanan bar Raba, "This [rule that all kinds must be in hand] has been stated only in a case in which one did not have all of them, but if he had them all, then one does not invalidate the other [if they are not bound together in a single handful]."
D. *To that proposition an objection was raised:* Among the four species that are joined in the *lulab*, two produce fruit, and two do not produce fruit. Those that produce fruit are to be joined to those that do not, and those that do not are to be joined to those that do. And one does not carry out the pertinent obligation concerning them unless all of them form a single bundle. And so it is in regard to Israel's pleasing God, that too takes place only when all of them form a single community, in line with this verse: "He who builds his chambers in heaven and has founded his community upon earth" (Amos 9:6).
E. *What we have here is a conflict of Tannaite formulations, for it has been taught on Tannaite authority:*
F. **The lulab, whether bound with others or not —**
G. R. Judah says, "If it is bound up, it is valid, and if it is not bound up, it is not valid" [T. Suk. 2:10A-B].
H. *What is the scriptural basis for the position of R. Judah?*
I. *By means of a verbal correspondence he draws an analogy because the word "taking" occurs both in the present context and in the setting of the bunch of hyssop [used in the purification rites of the person afflicted with the skin ailment, Lev. 14:4]. Just as in that context, what is required is that a bundle be made, so here too, what is required is that a bundle be made.*

J. *And rabbis?*

K. *They draw no such analogy established by the common appearance of the same word, "taking."*

L. *In accord with which of the two positions is the following, which has been taught on Tannaite authority:*

M. *The proper performance of the religious duty in regard to the lulab is to bind the species together, but if one has not done so, it is valid.*

N. *In accord with which party is that statement? Now this cannot be in accord with R. Judah, for if one has not bound the species together, why should the arrangement be valid?*

O. *And it can hardly accord with rabbis [vis à vis Judah], for why should it be an element of the religious duty [to do so at all, if they say one need not do so]?*

P. *Indeed, the statement accords with rabbis, and what is the sense of "religious duty"? It is on the count of, "This is my God and I will glorify him" (Ex. 15:2), which means one should be glorified before him through carrying out religious duties [in an especially felicitous manner, but if one does not do things exactly in that way, the action remains valid].*

See M. Menahot 3:5 XI.1.

33 Temurah

I found nothing that pertains in Bavli Temurah.

34 Keritot

M. Keritot 1:1-2 VI.9.

A. Said R. Hana bar Bizna said R. Simeon the Pious, "Any fast in which are not participating sinners among the Israelites is no fast.

B. "For lo, as to galbanum, the odor stinks, and yet it was included among the spices for the incense."

C. Abbayye said, "That is proved from here: 'and hath founded his vault upon the earth' (Amos 9:6)."

Amos 9:6 is again cited to prove that God treats all Israel as a single community.

35 Meilah

36 Tamid

37 NIDDAH

M. Niddah 3:1-2 IV. 2.

A. And so too, R. Hiyya b. Abba in the name of R. Yohanan said, *"This is the operative consideration in the view of R. Meir:* Since in the case of beasts and birds, the language of 'forming' is used just as it is used in the case of human beings ['And the Lord formed every beast...and every fowl' (Gen. 2:19), 'Then the Lord God formed man' (Gen. 2:7)]. [So the same rule applies to human beings and to abortions in the form of beasts or birds.]"

C. Said to him R. Ammi, "Then would a woman who aborts something in the form of mountain be unclean by reason of having given birth, since [the word 'form'] appears in that context, as it is said, 'For lo, he who forms the mountains and creates the wind' (Amos 4:13)."

D. *He said to him, "Now has the woman given birth to a mountain? What she aborts is a stone-shaped object, and that can be described as a lump."*

E. "Then would a woman who aborts wind by reason of having given birth, since [the word 'form'] appears in that context as much as in the context of forming a human being, as it is said, 'For lo, he who forms the mountains and creates the wind' (Amos 4:13). *And should you say it is not available for interpretation along these lines, since Scripture ought to have said, 'Forms mountains and wind,' but has written, 'and forms wind,' it must follow that the clause is indeed left open for interpretation."*

F. He said to him, "We draw an analogy from teachings of the Torah for the purpose of teachings of the Torah, but we do not draw an analogy for teachings of the Torah from teachings of tradition [e.g., prophecy]."

Amos's usage of "form" bears the inference that the shape of a mountain signifies an act of creation, so Ammi.

M. Nid. 10:1 III.4.

A. *Minyamin of Saqsanah was going on a journey to the town of Samuel. He considered making a practical ruling in accord with the position of Rab even in a case in which the woman had already produced a flow of blood, in the assumption that Rab made no distinction between one who had produced blood already and one who might. But he died while on the journey.*

B. *In regard to Rab Samuel cited the verse,* "There shall no mischief befall the righteous" (Prov. 12:21).

C. Said R. Hinena bar Shelamaya in the name of Rab, "As soon as a person's teeth fall out, his earning power is reduced: 'And I also have given you cleanness of teeth in all your cities and want of bread in all your places' (Amos 4:6)."

"Cleanness of teeth" refers to loss of teeth and consequent famine due to loss of earning power.

Index of Amos citations

1:1
    8
1:3
    16, 63
1:6
    16, 63, 77
1:9
    16, 77, 78
1:11
    41, 55, 98
1:21
    63
2:1
    101
2:4
    11
2:6
    3, 86, 102
2:9
    14, 20, 49, 73, 98, 114
2:10
    4
3:2
    108
3:6
    64
3:7
    4, 10, 18, 22, 30, 39, 43, 72, 97, 103
3:8
    22, 58, 82, 111
3:12
    23
3:15
    68, 86

4:1	8, 18, 84
4:2	101
4:3	69
4:4	30, 31
4:5	31, 32
4:6	116
4:7	1, 25, 26, 56, 72, 88, 89, 103
4:9	84
4:12	2, 25, 26, 82, 83, 84
4:13	27, 34, 35, 51, 77, 82, 92, 94, 102, 113, 116
4:14	51
5:1	59, 75
5:2	60, 81
5:4	64, 74
5:8	12, 23, 36, 37, 83
5:9	30
5:10	38
5:13	13
5:15	27, 42, 51, 64, 70, 77, 92
5:17	19
5:18	104

Index

5:19
      67, 103
5:25
      5, 92, 93
6:1
      45
6:2
      46
6:3
      46
6:4
      14, 15, 46, 85, 99
6:5
      46
6:6
      15, 46, 47, 50, 68, 85
6:7
      15, 47, 50, 68, 84, 85, 95, 99
6:9
      84
6:10
      76
6:11
      50, 74
6:13
      17
7:2
      112
7:5-6
      107
7:7
      53, 57, 76, 79, 99
7:8
      53, 76
7:10
      85
7:11
      85
7:14
      51, 65, 96
7:17
      13, 16, 95

8:3	71
8:5	101
8:7	101
8:10	45, 81, 87, 89, 90, 91, 109, 110
8:11	38, 39, 40, 70
8:12	2, 13
8:14	25, 42
8:17	3
9:1	6, 20, 29, 41, 54, 57, 76, 79
9:4	21
9:6	14, 36, 37, 51, 78, 94, 111, 114
9:7	7, 71, 90
9:11	60, 103
9:13	18, 42, 50, 56, 70
9:14	2
9:15	21
9:22ff	19

STUDIES IN JUDAISM
TITLES IN THE SERIES
PUBLISHED BY UNIVERSITY PRESS OF AMERICA

Judith Z. Abrams
The Babylonian Talmud: A Topical Guide, 2002.

Roger David Aus
Matthew 1-2 and the Virginal Conception: In Light of Palestinian and Hellenistic Judaic Traditions on the Birth of Israel's First Redeemer, Moses, 2004.

My Name Is "Legion": Palestinian Judaic Traditions in Mark 5:1-20 and Other Gospel Texts, 2003.

Alan L. Berger, Harry James Cargas, and Susan E. Nowak
The Continuing Agony: From the Carmelite Convent to the Crosses at Auschwitz, 2004.

S. Daniel Breslauer
Creating a Judaism without Religion: A Postmodern Jewish Possibility, 2001.

Bruce Chilton
Targumic Approaches to the Gospels: Essays in the Mutual Definition of Judaism and Christianity, 1986.

David Ellenson
Tradition in Transition: Orthodoxy, Halakhah, and the Boundaries of Modern Jewish Identity, 1989.

Paul V. M. Flesher
New Perspectives on Ancient Judaism, Volume 5: Society and Literature in Analysis, 1990.

Marvin Fox
Collected Essays on Philosophy and on Judaism, Volume One: Greek Philosophy, Maimonides, 2003.

Collected Essays on Philosophy and on Judaism, Volume Two: Some Philosophers, 2003.

Collected Essays on Philosophy and on Judaism, Volume Three: Ethics, Reflections, 2003.

Zev Garber
Methodology in the Academic Teaching of Judaism, 1986.

Zev Garber, Alan L. Berger, and Richard Libowitz
Methodology in the Academic Teaching of the Holocaust, 1988.

Abraham Gross
Spirituality and Law: Courting Martyrdom in Christianity and Judaism, 2005.

Harold S. Himmelfarb and Sergio DellaPergola
Jewish Education Worldwide: Cross-Cultural Perspectives, 1989.

William Kluback
The Idea of Humanity: Hermann Cohen's Legacy to Philosophy and Theology, 1987.

Samuel Morell
Studies in the Judicial Methodology of Rabbi David ibn Abi Zimra, 2004.

Jacob Neusner
Amos in Talmud and Midrash, 2006.

Ancient Israel, Judaism, and Christianity in Contemporary Perspective, 2006.

The Aggadic Role in Halakhic Discourses: Volume I, 2001.

The Aggadic Role in Halakhic Discourses: Volume II, 2001.

The Aggadic Role in Halakhic Discourses: Volume III, 2001.

Analysis and Argumentation in Rabbinic Judaism, 2003.

Analytical Templates of the Bavli, 2006.

Ancient Judaism and Modern Category-Formation: "Judaism," "Midrash," "Messianism," and Canon in the Past Quarter Century, 1986.

Canon and Connection: Intertextuality in Judaism, 1987.

Chapters in the Formative History of Judaism. 2006

Dual Discourse, Single Judaism, 2001.

The Emergence of Judaism: Jewish Religion in Response to the Critical Issues of the First Six Centuries, 2000.

First Principles of Systemic Analysis: The Case of Judaism within the History of Religion, 1988.

The Halakhah and the Aggadah, 2001.

Halakhic Hermeneutics, 2003.

Halakhic Theology: A Sourcebook, 2006.

The Hermeneutics of Rabbinic Category Formations, 2001.

Hosea in Talmud and Midrash, 2006.

How Important Was the Destruction of the Second Temple in the Formation of Rabbinic Judaism? 2006.

How Not to Study Judaism, Examples and Counter-Examples, Volume One: Parables, Rabbinic Narratives, Rabbis' Biographies, Rabbis' Disputes, 2004.

How Not to Study Judaism, Examples and Counter-Examples, Volume Two: Ethnicity and Identity versus Culture and

Religion, How Not to Write a Book on Judaism, Point and Counterpoint, 2004.

How the Halakhah Unfolds: Moed Qatan in the Mishnah, ToseftaYerushalmi and Bavli, 2006.

The Implicit Norms of Rabbinic Judaism. 2006.

Intellectual Templates of the Law of Judaism, 2006.

Is Scripture the Origin of the Halakhah? 2005.

Israel and Iran in Talmudic Times: A Political History, 1986.

Israel's Politics in Sasanian Iran: Self-Government in Talmudic Times, 1986.

Jeremiah in Talmud and Midrash: A Source Book, 2006.

Judaism in Monologue and Dialogue, 2005.

Major Trends in Formative Judaism, Fourth Series, 2002.

Major Trends in Formative Judaism, Fifth Series, 2002.

Messiah in Context: Israel's History and Destiny in Formative Judaism, 1988.

Micah and Joel in Talmud and Midrash, 2006.

The Native Category - Formations of the Aggadah: The Later Midrash-Compilations - Volume I, 2000.

The Native Category - Formations of the Aggadah: The Earlier Midrash-Compilations - Volume II, 2000.

Paradigms in Passage: Patterns of Change in the Contemporary Study of Judaism, 1988.

Parsing the Torah, 2005.

Praxis and Parable: The Divergent Discourses of Rabbinic Judaism, 2006.

Rabbi Jeremiah, 2006.

Reading Scripture with the Rabbis: The Five Books of Moses, 2006.

The Religious Study of Judaism: Description, Analysis and Interpretation, Volume 1, 1986.

The Religious Study of Judaism: Description, Analysis, Interpretation, Volume 2, 1986.

The Religious Study of Judaism: Context, Text, Circumstance, Volume 3, 1987.

The Religious Study of Judaism: Description, Analysis, Interpretation, Volume 4: Ideas of History, Ethics, Ontology, and Religion in Formative Judaism, 1988.

Struggle for the Jewish Mind: Debates and Disputes on Judaism Then and Now, 1988.

The Talmud Law, Theology, Narrative: A Sourcebook, 2005.

Talmud Torah: Ways to God's Presence through Learning: An Exercise in Practical Theology, 2002.

Texts Without Boundaries: Protocols of Non-Documentary Writing in the Rabbinic Canon: Volume I: The Mishnah, Tractate Abot, and the Tosefta, 2002.

Texts Without Boundaries: Protocols of Non-Documentary Writing in the Rabbinic Canon: Volume II: Sifra and Sifré to Numbers, 2002.

Texts Without Boundaries: Protocols of Non-Documentary Writing in the Rabbinic Canon: Volume III: Sifré to Deuteronomy and Mekhilta Attributed to Rabbi Ishmael, 2002.

Texts Without Boundaries: Protocols of Non-Documentary Writing in the Rabbinic Canon: Volume IV: Leviticus Rabbah, 2002.

A Theological Commentary to the Midrash - Volume I: Pesiqta deRab Kahana, 2001.

A Theological Commentary to the Midrash - Volume II: Genesis Raba, 2001.

A Theological Commentary to the Midrash - Volume III: Song of Songs Rabbah, 2001.

A Theological Commentary to the Midrash - Volume IV: Leviticus Rabbah, 2001.

A Theological Commentary to the Midrash - Volume V: Lamentations Rabbati, 2001.

A Theological Commentary to the Midrash - Volume VI: Ruth Rabbah and Esther Rabbah, 2001.

A Theological Commentary to the Midrash - Volume VII: Sifra, 2001.

A Theological Commentary to the Midrash - Volume VIII: Sifré to Numbers and Sifré to Deuteronomy, 2001.

A Theological Commentary to the Midrash - Volume IX: Mekhilta Attributed to Rabbi Ishmael, 2001.

Theological Dictionary of Rabbinic Judaism: Part One: Principal Theological Categories, 2005.

Theological Dictionary of Rabbinic Judaism: Part Two: Making Connections and Building Constructions, 2005.

Theological Dictionary of Rabbinic Judaism: Part Three: Models of Analysis, Explanation, and Anticipation, 2005.

The Theological Foundations of Rabbinic Midrash, 2006.

Theology of Normative Judaism: A Source Book, 2005.

Theology in Action: How the Rabbis of the Talmud Present Theology (Aggadah) in the Medium of the Law (Halakhah). An Anthology, 2006

The Torah and the Halakhah: The Four Relationships, 2003.

The Unity of Rabbinic Discourse: Volume I: Aggadah in the Halakhah, 2001.

The Unity of Rabbinic Discourse: Volume II: Halakhah in the Aggadah, 2001.

The Unity of Rabbinic Discourse: Volume III: Halakhah and Aggadah in Concert, 2001.

The Vitality of Rabbinic Imagination: The Mishnah Against the Bible and Qumran, 2005.

Who, Where and What is "Israel?": Zionist Perspectives on Israeli and American Judaism, 1989.

The Wonder-Working Lawyers of Talmudic Babylonia: The Theory and Practice of Judaism in its Formative Age, 1987.

Jacob Neusner and Ernest S. Frerichs
New Perspectives on Ancient Judaism, Volume 2: Judaic and Christian Interpretation of Texts: Contents and Contexts, 1987.

New Perspectives on Ancient Judaism, Volume 3: Judaic and Christian Interpretation of Texts: Contents and Contexts, 1987.

Jacob Neusner and James F. Strange
Religious Texts and Material Contexts, 2001.

David Novak and Norbert M. Samuelson
Creation and the End of Days: Judaism and Scientific Cosmology, 1986.
Proceedings of the Academy for Jewish Philosophy, 1990.

Risto Nurmela
The Mouth of the Lord Has Spoken: Inner-Biblical Allusions in Second and Third Isaiah, 2006.

Aaron D. Panken
The Rhetoric of Innovation: Self-Conscious Legal Change in Rabbinic Literature, 2005.

Norbert M. Samuelson
Studies in Jewish Philosophy: Collected Essays of the Academy for Jewish Philosophy, 1980-1985, 1987.

Benjamin Edidin Scolnic
Alcimus, Enemy of the Maccabees, 2004.

If the Egyptians Drowned in the Red Sea Where are Pharaoh's Chariots?: Exploring the Historical Dimension of the Bible, 2005.

Rivka Ulmer
Pesiqta Rabbati: A Synoptic Edition of Pesiqta Rabbati Based upon all Extant Manuscripts and the Editio Princeps, Volume III, 2002.

Manfred H. Vogel
A Quest for a Theology of Judaism: The Divine, the Human and the Ethical Dimensions in the Structure-of-Faith of Judaism Essays in Constructive, 1987.

Anita Weiner
Renewal: Reconnecting Soviet Jewry to the Soviet People: A Decade of American Jewish Joint Distribution Committee (AJJDC) Activities in the Former Soviet Union 1988-1998, 2003.

Eugene Weiner and Anita Weiner
Israel-A Precarious Sanctuary: War, Death and the Jewish People, 1989.

The Martyr's Conviction: A Sociological Analysis, 2002.

Leslie S. Wilson
The Serpent Symbol in the Ancient Near East: Nahash and Asherah: Death, Life, and Healing, 2001.

www.ingramcontent.com/pod-product-compliance
Lightning Source LLC
Chambersburg PA
CBHW021129300426
44113CB00006B/346